Christine Shaw moved to Dorset in 1982, reluctantly dragging her feet over the eastern boundary from busy Hampshire. Now, she can't imagine living anywhere else, and as well as writing *Dorset for Free* she is also the author of the highly successful *Dorset Garden Guide*.

Her pleasure in her adopted county is shared in *Dorset for Free*. You need nothing to enjoy it with her, save a willingness to explore and seek out some of the hundreds of ideas contained in the book.

Christine's early years in the county were a voyage of discovery with her two children, and many of the places and pleasures they enjoyed then have found their way into the book. "It's simple Dorset philosophy", says Christine. "Who needs to be born with a silver spoon, when they can have Golden Cap in their sights any day of the year?"

Following page
The Customs House, Poole

Christine Shaw

DORSET FOR FREE

Illustrations by Graham Shaw

THE DOVECOTE PRESS

For Toby and Daniel
May the best things in life always be free

First published in 1992 by The Dovecote Press Ltd
Stanbridge, Wimborne, Dorset BH21 4JD

ISBN 1 874336 00 8
© Christine Shaw 1992
Illustrations © Graham Shaw 1992

Designed by Humphrey Stone
Phototypeset by The Typesetting Bureau,
Wimborne, Dorset
Printed and bound by Biddles Ltd,
Guildford and King's Lynn

CONTENTS

INTRODUCTION

Dorset deservedly holds a place well to the top of the tourist league. Holidays can be packed with excitement and exploration; every hour used to capacity, however you prefer to fill your time. But it all costs money; or does it?

Let us assume, if you have a car, that you have budgeted for petrol and parking charges on a modest scale. If you are relying on public transport, fares have been put aside. Whether you are free to move around this rural county at will, or are confined to one area, take heart: there is plenty to do and see — and it's free.

Dorset for free! There's a lot of it. The following pages contain more than 150 ideas for visits, entertainments, and ways of discovering the county with a light heart instead of a light purse.

Wherever you are staying, visit the local Tourist Information Centre without delay. They will have the latest information on precise dates and times of events planned during your stay, and you will find them able and willing to help make your holiday a success.

If you are relying on public transport, get details of an Explorer Go-anywhere One-day ticket. Family tickets or singles are available. This gives unlimited travel on any Wilts & Dorset buses for a day, changing as often as you like. Information can be found at Tourist Information Centres, Bus Stations, or telephone 0202-673555.

The only way to really discover and appreciate Dorset's towns is on foot. The Town Trails are the result of painstaking research by many, and I am grateful to the following for permission to reproduce their work here: The Beaminster Society (Marie Eedle); Blandford Forum Civic Society; Bridport Civic Society; Christchurch Borough Council; Dorset County Council (Monmouth Trail); Shaftesbury & District Tourism Association; Sherborne Town Guide (Alphabet & Image Ltd); Swanage Town Council; Weymouth Civic Society; Wimborne Civic Society.

The information given is up-to-date at the time of going to press. If you find any changes, or would like us to add any facility you may have discovered for yourself, write to Dorset for Free, Dovecote Press Ltd, Stanbridge, Wimborne BH21 4JD. Your comments will be welcome.

Please remember the Country Code and, for your own safety, heed advice on exploring our Heritage Coast. Enjoy Dorset, and please return.

Christine Shaw
Charminster

Corfe Castle.

ANCIENT SITES

Dorset is rich in earthworks, hillforts, and other ancient sites. All are in areas of beautiful countryside, often with wide ranging views over the county. I have used the Ordnance Survey Landranger 1:50,000 series maps and grid references, since many can be approached from several different directions. The map sheet number is given in brackets, and maps are available for reference in the County Library at Dorchester. Where sites are near a major road, I have included more specific directions.

Ackling Dyke
(184) 015163. The route of one of the major Roman roads crossing the county is marked by this lengthy earthwork. It begins east of Dorchester near Hardy's cottage, running north and east through Badbury Rings to Old Sarum, outside Salisbury.

In the north of the county, where it crosses the B3081 from Cranborne to Sixpenny Handley at Bottlebrush Down, is an easy spot to begin explorations. Nearby there is a group of 31 Bronze Age barrows at Oakley Down.

Badbury Rings
(195) 964030. Off B3082 Wimborne Minster to Blandford Forum. Badbury Rings is recognised as one of the finest Iron Age hill forts in southern England. It is now owned by the National Trust, and the entrance to the Rings is off the fine Beech Avenue leading to Kingston Lacy house. Point to point races are held at the Rings on four Saturdays early in the year, and at these times the car park is closed to visitors.

Bokerly Ditch
(184) 032199. South of the A354 Blandford Forum/Salisbury road. Bokerly Ditch (4th century) was built as a defence against the Saxons across the north eastern boundary of the county, and crosses Ackling

Dyke at that point. It is the county boundary between Dorset and Hampshire, overlooking the nature reserve of Martin Down. It can be explored from the villages of Martin or Pentridge.

Cerne Giant

(194) 665017. Just north of Cerne Abbas on the A 352 Dorchester to Sherborne road is a lay-by from which there is an excellent view of this striding chalk figure.

To see him at close quarters, walk along Abbey Street in the village and through the abbey grounds, where a path cuts up through the trees to the top of the hill.

The Giant stands some 180' high, and speculation as to his purpose and origin still continues. He is cleaned and re-chalked at regular intervals, although in the mid 19th century the local clergy opposed this operation as being likely to corrupt the participants!

Coneys Castle

(193) 372975. North of Charmouth.

A small Iron Age fort. There is parking to the north, towards Fishpond Bottom. Glorious for picnics, with lovely views out over the Marshwood Vale.

Dorset Cursus

(195) 994139, at Gussage Hill.

On the southern edge of the Cranborne Chase, the six mile long Dorset Cursus has to a large extent been ploughed out. Originally two banks and ditches running parallel to each other, dating from about 3,000 BC.

To search for traces of the Cursus, start at Bottlebrush Down on the B3081 where it can be seen as an earthwork on either side of the road. At Thickthorn Down on the A354 can be seen two long barrows at the south western end of the Cursus.

Eggardon Hillfort

(194) 543946. Take the Roman road right off the A35 travelling from Dorchester to Bridport, just before Winterbourne Abbas.

Eggardon hillfort at Askerswell provides fine views across countryside to the coast. Surrounded by three ramparts and two ditches for much of the circumference, this 20 acre site is now owned by the National Trust.

Hambledon Hill

(194) 845125. Near Child Okeford.

Footpaths approach this fort from both east and west. It is the most impressive in the county, with excellent walking and views.

The Clubmen fought their last stand on Hambledon in 1645. Countrymen armed only with stout clubs, they bitterly opposed the Civil War and bravely faced Oliver Cromwell's army. but despite having superior numbers they were overwhelmed.

Hod Hill

(194) 857106. North west of Stourpaine.

One mile away from Hambledon Hill, and owned by the National Trust. Again, excellent walking and views.

This Iron Age hillfort contains a Roman fort, and at one time housed nearly 1,000 men including cavalry. The enclosure of Hod is extensive, the largest of any in Dorset. It makes an excellent day out, linked with neighbouring Hambledon Hill.

Kingston Russell Stone Circle

(194) 578878. North of Abbotsbury.

A footpath passes close by the Grey Mare and Colts, a Neolithic long barrow, or it is possible to approach from other directions to find the stone circle. The stones are no longer standing - but the site has the fascination and poses the questions of all stone circles.

Knowlton Rings

(195) 024104. Off B3078 Wimborne Minster to Cranborne.

A ruined church is surrounded by single rampart and ditch, the latter being the only surviving earthwork on the site of a large collection of henge monuments and a deserted medieval village. Possibly the Rings were used for religious ceremonies, and the church later built to bring Christianity to the site.

Knowlton Church and Rings.

Lamberts Castle
(193) 371988. North of Charmouth.

Iron Age fort owned by the National Trust. It is close to Coneys Castle, and there is a car park off the B3165.

Maiden Castle
(194) 668885. 2 miles south west of Dorchester town centre.

Maiden Castle, "the most massively defended hillfort in Dorset", enjoys commanding views over the town. Extensive archaeological digs have established Neolithic, Early Iron Age and Roman occupations, and many of the finds can be seen in Dorset County Museum.

Sir Mortimer Wheeler carried out excavations in the 1930's, and uncovered a war cemetery of 34 people. Many had been put to the sword, and one had a Roman arrowhead embedded in his spine.

There are the remains of a small Roman temple on the ramparts.

Maumbury Rings

(194) 690899. Beyond Dorchester South railway station, by the traffic lights on the Weymouth road.

This amphitheatre was built in about 2500 BC, and has been used for many different purposes over the centuries. As late as 1767 there were public hangings at Maumbury Rings, the gallows having been removed from its earlier site in South Walks. The Rings were traditionally used for large gatherings in the town, when crowds of 10,000 or more filled the grassy banks.

Pilsdon Pen

(193) 413013. South west of Broadwindsor, near Beaminster.

Pilsdon's Iron Age fort is the second highest point in Dorset at 277 metres. Together with neighbouring Lewesdon (279 metres) the hills have splendid views over the Marshwood Vale. Owned by the National Trust. Park beside Pilsdon, and follow the path to the turf ramparts.

Rawlsbury

(194) 767058. South east of Hazelbury Bryan. A small hill fort just west of Bulbarrrow, in extremely pretty surrounding landscape.

COAST

Two stretches of Heritage Coast edge Dorset: Purbeck runs from Poole Harbour nearly into Weymouth, and West Dorset stretches from Portland along Chesil Bank to Lyme Bay.

Sandy bays, pebble shoals, rocks and cliffs - Dorset has them all. The character of the coast can change dramatically from one mile to the next. On a fine day, stand on Weymouth promenade and look round the sweep of the bay and out to the cliffs to the east; pause on Portland, and admire the line of Chesil disappearing to the west.

A Heritage Coast is one considered worthy of conservation, where visitors are encouraged to enjoy the coastline in ways which do not endanger its conservation. Informative leaflets detailing 300 miles of waymarked paths are freely available from Tourist Information Centres.

A large area to the east of Lulworth Cove is covered by the Army firing ranges. There are prominent notices at all vehicular and pedestrian access points giving clear information as to whether or not the ranges are open. They are usually open during main holiday periods. When walking, follow the clearly waymarked paths and OBSERVE ALL WARNING SIGNS. The range walks give access to wonderful stretches of coast, but the dangers of straying from the paths should be recognised by all.

Anvil Point Lighthouse, Swanage
The lighthouse is open from Easter to September, from 11am until one hour before sunset. It is closed in foggy weather. If you are travelling a long distance, 'phone 0929-422146 to check on opening arrangements for the day. There is no charge, but donations can be made.

Black Ven and the Spittles
Just east of Lyme Regis, this is an interesting area of meadows and scrub, with overgrown landslips. There is a small car park,and a cliff

walk above Black Ven which is part of the Dorset Coast Path. On the shore can still be found the fossils for which the area is famous, but the cliffs must not be climbed or excavated – heed all warnings.

Bournemouth

Dorset's largest beach resort. Seven miles long, Bournemouth's sandy beach is considered to be one of the finest in Europe. Dog and pollution free, it is sifted, swept and cleansed daily. Fresh sand is pumped ashore from time to time to increase the play area, and freshwater showers installed along the promenade are a welcome facility.

Bournemouth's beach is just a step away from the bustling and lively town centre. The facilities are all one would expect in a major seaside town, with events and attractions for all the family throughout the summer months.

The neighbouring beaches at Boscombe and Southbourne are equally beautiful, but these are smaller centres for those who prefer to leave the hustle of the main resort behind.

Burton Bradstock

National Trust area of shingle beach accessible from a grass car park, just east of Bridport. There are riverside and cliff walks through 83 acres.

Charmouth and Heritage Coast Centre

Not as well known as some of the bigger resorts, but nevertheless enjoyable. East and West Beaches are divided by the River Char. East Beach stretches 2 miles to Golden Cap, while West Beach runs almost into Lyme Regis. At low tide there is excellent walking on the sandy bay, and it is only about a mile into Lyme. Care *must* be taken with the tides. It is very easy to be trapped below the cliffs.

The Blue Lias cliffs on either side are renowned for deposits of fossils, particularly ammonites, a flat spiral shellfish. Fossil-hunting can be fun; also dangerous, if unstable cliffs are excavated.

The Heritage Coast Centre is open from June to September, on the upper floors of an old cement works in Lower Sea Lane. Exhibits include information on cliffs, fossils and the coast, the layout of footpaths within the surrounding area, and some local history. There is no charge, but the Centre relies on donations for its maintenance.

Chesil Bank/The Fleet

This ridge of shingle and pebbles is unique in Europe. It stretches 15 miles from Portland at its eastern end through to West Bay, at Bridport, and for 8 of those miles traps behind it a lagoon known as The Fleet. The Chesil Management Scheme has an Information Centre in the Portland Harbour car park during the summer season, from where there is easy access onto the Bank.

Chesil Bank is dangerous for swimming, even for the very experienced, but is recognised as one of the finest fishing beaches in Britain. Bird watchers and naturalists also find plenty to see along this stretch of the coast.

The Fleet is one of the oldest nature reserves in Britain.

Church Ope Cove, Portland

Off Church Ope Road on the east side of Portland. Nearby Rufus Castle, 15th century ruins, has 7 feet thick walls pierced by archery slits and circular gun ports.

The cove is reached by a descent of 125 steps, and was a beach much used by smugglers. It is a pebble beach, and a favourite for swimmers. On the way to the cove bear right to St Andrews Church, and you will be able to find a tombstone with a skull and crossbones, and another dedicated to "John the Bad".

Dancing Ledge

Midway between Anvil Point and St Aldhelm's Head, an area of magnificent scenery. It is a favourite picnic spot, whether for a warm summer laze or hearty winter blow. There are footpaths from Langton Matravers, or Worth Matravers inland, and it is on the route of the Dorset Coast Path.

Dorset Coast Path

This well marked route follows the coast for most of its length, from Lyme Regis to Poole Harbour. The inland route, from West Bexington to Osmington Mills, passes near Maiden Castle. The entire length affords panoramic views of coast and county.

Through the military ranges between Lulworth Cove and Kimmeridge use of the path is limited usually to week-ends and holiday periods. See local warning signs. For accurate information on a day-to-day basis, 'phone Bindon Abbey 462721.

Durdle Door

Of all the rock formations along the Dorset coast this is probably the most impressive and certainly the most well known. The natural rock arch stands 40 feet clear of the sea between two small beaches. There is a large car park at the top of the cliff, but for the more energetic it can be reached on foot from West Lulworth, over Hambury Tout to Man o' War Cove and beyond.

Hengistbury Head

Bordering Christchurch Harbour, a heath land nature reserve with sandy shores. There are wonderful views of the coast and harbour, and the walking is good.

Kimmeridge

The Purbeck Marine Reserve at Kimmeridge is reached along a toll road. There is a Visitor Centre and car park at Kimmeridge Bay. The 'Nodding Donkey' stands at the head of a small oil well nearby.

The shale ledges at Kimmeridge make exploration fascinating. This is a bay for the 'doer. not the sunbather.

Lulworth Cove and the Fossil Forest

The basin of Lulworth Cove, with its narrow sea entrance, forms a tiny natural harbour. Nearby Stair Hole has interesting rock strata, and to the east of the cove is the Fossil Forest. This latter is only accessible at weekends because it is within the Army firing ranges, but is well worth the walk.

Lyme Regis

This charming seaside town is usually remembered either as the start-ing point for the Monmouth rebellion in 1685, or for the filming of 'The French Lieutenant's Woman'.

The Cobb harbour wall (13th century) is now clad in Portland stone, but until Regency times it consisted of 'cow stones' — large round boulders — stacked inside an oak casing.

There are small beaches suitable for bathing, and some excellent walking around the area. The nearby cliffs are the haunt of fossil

The Cobb, Lyme Regis.

hunters, and it was at Black Ven (to the east) that a nichthyosaurus was found. It is now on display in the Natural History Museum in London. Fossils still come to light, but hunting is best confined to the beach. The unstable cliff formations are dangerous, and should be left well alone.

The Undercliff, a National Trust Reserve, is to the west of the town. An area of wooded landslips, there is a public footpath running through it for those intent on a long walk

Mudeford Quay

East of Christchurch, at the entrance to the harbour. This is the centre of the local fishing industry, with always something happening of interest to the visitor. It is a popular sailing centre, and a number of dinghy championships are held here each year. There are good swimming beaches nearby, and an inshore lifeboat base.

Poole Harbour and Quay

Poole Harbour is now believed to be the largest natural harbour in the world. It used to come second to Sydney in Australia, but since much of that has now been reclaimed Poole tops the table. There may not be the same sunshine record, but the harbour is nevertheless an interesting stretch of the Dorset coastline. Unlike neighbouring Bournemouth, there are no vast beaches of sand. Instead, the bustling harbour and quayside give the more active holidaymaker plenty to see and do.

This centuries-old port is still a centre both for large commercial shipping, including cross channel ferries, and yachtsmen of all ages who use the extensive inland waters as well as venturing further out into the English Channel.

Portland Bill and Lighthouse

Portland Bill, the southernmost tip of Portland, is a conservation area with caves, rock pools and ledges for exploration. It is popular with visitors, always crowded in the summer, and there is a large car park.

The shipping lanes are very busy, both with Royal Navy vessels and the local fishing fleets. The dangerous waters of the Portland Race and the Shambles make the lighthouse a necessity.

The lighthouse, built in 1906, is open from 11 am to one hour before sunset. It is closed to the public in fog.

Ringstead Bay

Turn right off the A353 Weymouth/Warmwell road, just before the village of Poxwell. One road leads up onto the clifftop, owned by the National Trust, where there is plenty of parking. There are steep paths (slippery when wet) leading down to Ringstead Bay.

The bay itself is stoney, backed by the cliffs, but is usually very quiet even at peak holiday times.

The lower road leads right down to the shore, where there is a car park (fee) and small shop.

St Aldhelm's Head

An isolated Norman chapel and nearby coastguards' cottages can be reached on foot from Worth Matravers. There are wonderful coastal views.

Portland Bill and Lighthouse.

Studland Beach

Open all year, there is a National Trust car park available from 9am to 8pm. Parking charges are highest in July and August.

The pretty village of Studland just north of Swanage is often the scene of long traffic queues in the summer, but the wait is worth it to enjoy the miles of glorious sand and dunes. The bathing is excellent, with views out over the Channel and Poole Harbour.

Studland Heath is a Nature Conservancy Council reserve, with several public paths and two nature trails.

West Bay, Bridport

The 'harbour' end of Bridport, standing at the mouth of the River Brit. There are usually working fishing boats. This is an excellent diving centre, as ships failing to clear Portland Bill in storms invariably came to grief nearby. Among the wrecks here – known locally as 'Deadman's Bay' – are ships of the Spanish Armada. There is good walking, particularly for those with an interest in geology.

Weymouth Beach
This wide sweep of bay backed by its lovely Esplanade has been awarded the Blue Flag for cleanliness. A popular resort in the summer months, it is equally enjoyable when the holiday crowds have gone home and the coastline is swept by stiff winds.

Weymouth Old Harbour
Bordered by Custom House Quay, Cove Row and Trinity Road. Many buildings are in commercial use, but the area is still very attractive. Local fishing boats, visiting small craft, and the Condor Hydrofoil can be seen.

There is parking on the Quay – crowded in summer – and you may then walk along to the Town Bridge to cross over to Cove Row/Trinity Road. (See Weymouth Town Trails.)

Worbarrow Bay
If you like a walk, this beautiful bay is accessible only on foot via the deserted village of Tyneham. It is surrounded by spectacular cliffs, including the delightfully named Worbarrow Tout.

COUNTRY PARKS

Dorset's five country parks vary in character and situation, from Lodmoor close to Weymouth's busy centre, to Durlston high on the Purbeck cliffs. All the parks cater for visitors, with car parking and other facilities, including information centres.

Avon Forest

The park is divided into three areas, all with parking. Access to the North Park and Visitor Centre is from the A31 at Woolsbridge Roundabout between Ashley Heath and Ferndown. South Park lies off Boundary Lane close to the A338 into Bournemouth, with Matchams View nearby. Avon Forest Park is open all year. The Visitor Centre opens from early February to the end of September every day 10.30 am – 5 pm. For further information tel: 0425-478082.

580 acres of heathland and pine woodland make Avon Forest the largest country park in Dorset. North Park has plenty of picnic spots and waymarked trails. South Park has grass meadows and wildflowers; two ancient burial mounds provide vantage points from which to enjoy the surrounding countryside. Matchams View, the smallest area, sits at the head of the Avon Valley, with a woodland walk down to an old railway cutting.

The park is a haven for the conservation of wildlife, the story of which is presented in a slide show and through interesting displays in the Visitor Centre. Events programmes are also available here, and give details of the 'specials' held throughout the year such as guided walks, treasure hunts, and study sessions.

The Globe, Durlston Country Park, Swanage.

Durlston

5 minutes drive from the centre of Swanage, and well signposted. There is a Park Centre. Enquiries can be made to the Head Warden, tel: 0929 424443.

Durlston is within the Purbeck Heritage Coast and Area of Outstanding Natural Beauty, and became Dorset's first country park in 1973.

The park's origins belong to George Burt, who was described by Thomas Hardy as 'the King of Swanage'. George Burt bought the estate which included Durlston Head in 1864, and was full of imaginative ideas for its development. It was Burt who created woods, paths and seats, and a Castle. He also devised the Great Globe of Portland stone which was placed below the Castle, and which still fascinates visitors today.

Covering 300 acres, there are varied habitats for wildlife such as heath and scrub, grasslands and coppices. Sheer Portland limestone cliffs drop to the sea, and safe paths provide an opportunity to watch colonies of noisy seabirds. The lucky may see dolphins as they bask offshore, and pilot whales are sited several times a year.

Wildflowers include several rare orchids, and two of the rarer butterflies which may be spotted are the Chalkhill and Adonis Blue.

Lodmoor

A353 Preston Beach Road, 1 mile by car from Weymouth Town Centre, or a 15 minute stroll through Greenhill Gardens. There is a large car park (small charge). Buses run every 5 minutes from Weymouth King's Statue, with a return stop just outside the car park entrance. After 4.30 pm the bus service is hourly. The Information Centre is open weekends and Bank Holidays from Easter to June; 7 days a week in July and August.

This 350 acre sea level site is set in a valley, only yards from Weymouth Bay and Greenhill Beach. It is a good place to picnic, with tables and benches set up for public use. There are small gardens.

The adjacent RSPB Lodmoor Reserve has a footpath through the saltmarsh lake, and display boards provide information on the many birds to be seen. There are picnic tables here, too, for keen bird spotters.

Moors Valley

Horton Road, Ashley Heath. Open daily, dawn to dusk. Events programmes and other information from Warden's Office 0425-470721. Tea room open 10.30 - 5pm every day.

Moors Valley Country Park, developed jointly by the District Council and Forestry Commission, has become popular as the ideal spot for families on a day out. There is plenty to do and see, whatever your age.

Children can let off steam on the narrow gauge railway (for which there is a small charge), and romp in the adventure playgrounds. Mum and Dad may prefer a quiet river or lakeside walk – there are two 9 acre lakes – or a walk within the pinewoods of St Leonard's Forest, where the tangy scent of needles being crushed underfoot provides nature's own aromatherapy.

Two rivers, the Moors and the Crane, run through the park, creating an interesting wildlife habitat to study, or just to relax and enjoy.

Special events are held frequently throughout the year. The Visitors' Centre, a picturesque 16th century barn, provides further information, as well as housing displays and exhibitions which change throughout the seasons. A team of Countryside Wardens will answer queries or provide help during your visit.

Upton

Follow the brown tourist signs on the south side of the A35, approximately 4 miles from the centre of Poole. There is a regular service from Poole bus station. Open every day from 9 am to dusk. Refreshments are available. (Entrance is usually free, but an admission charge may operate occasionally when special events are being held.)

The Country Heritage Centre is open 10.30 am to 5 pm from 1 May to 30 September; 10.30 am to 5 pm (or dusk of earlier) from 1 October to 30 April, but NOT Thursdays.

Upton is a peaceful country estate with formal gardens, farmland and woodland, on the edge of Poole Harbour. The estate surrounds Upton House, a lovely 19th century building, which was given to Poole by the Llewellin family in 1957. The upper floors are used as offices, but parts of the ground floor are open to the public on Sunday afternoons. The house is surrounded by formal gardens of trees, shrubs, roses, heather beds and herbaceous borders.   Permanent exhibitions and displays can be found in the Country Heritage Centre in the old stable block.

The shores of Poole harbour form one boundary to the park, with areas of saltmarsh which are ideal for bird watching. There is a hide, and two boardwalks which allow the public easy access to these areas.

COUNTRYSIDE

Most of Dorset is beautiful countryside, so any selection has to be a personal choice. The following are initial ideas — but it is up to you to get off the beaten track and discover favourite spots of your own; hidden places to which you can perhaps return year after year, in the gleeful knowledge that no-one else seems to have discovered them.

Arne RSPB Reserve
The small village of Arne is close to the edge of Poole harbour, and 1,200 acres of the surrounding heathland are an RSPB nature reserve. Turn for Arne off the A351 to Swanage, half a mile south of Wareham.

Most of the Reserve is not open to the public, but from a car park just south of the village a track leads to Shipstal Point on the shores of Poole harbour, where there is public access at all times. The half hour walk runs through woods and part of the Reserve, to a public hide just north of Shipstal Point. There are magnificent views across the harbour. Toilets. .

Ballard Down
Between Studland and Swanage, this could either be coast or country. As you are up off the beaches, I have included it in the latter. Nevertheless there are splendid sea views, and excellent walking.

Bulbarrow
The third highest point in Dorset, so views are wide on all sides. The nearby Ibberton Hill picnic site is popular, with car park. The most direct route from the south is the A354 Dorchester to Blandford road, turn left at Winterborne Whitechurch for Milton Abbas, and head for Hazelbury Bryan.

Delph Wood
Just south of Merley on the Wimborne/Poole road. Nature trail

around 24 acre woods with a bog, ponds etc. Car park.

Dorset Ridgeway
Runs for 12 miles east/west, to the south of Dorchester. At one time there were between 400 – 500 Bronze Age barrows along this stretch, one of the highest concentrations in the country. It is possible to walk the entire length, and enjoy the views. A good area to join the Ridgway is above Preston off Coombe Valley Road, where the path leads west through Bincombe.

Duncliffe Hill
2 miles west of Shaftesbury, and from the top you can see Devon, Somerset and Wiltshire. The woods are criss-crossed with footpaths.

Fontmell Down
Between Blandford and Shaftesbury. This is an area of chalk downland owned by the National Trust, and overlooks the Blackmore Vale to the west. There is a car park at the top of Spread Eagle Hill and at Compton Abbas airfield. Fontmell Down was bought by public appeal to commemorate the Dorset of Thomas Hardy, whose books describe the county in such detail.

Garston Wood RSPB Reserve
Just north of Sixpenny Handley off the main A 354 Salisbury/Blandford road. There is access at all times from a small car park. For more information on RSPB reserves, 'phone 0929-53360.

  The reserve protects a small part of the once extensive woodlands of the Cranborne Chase, and is particularly beautiful at bluebell time.

Golden Cap
The highest cliffs on the south coast give splendid views across this National Trust estate. The area is superb for walking, with miles of marked paths giving access to Charmouth, Chideock and Seatown. Start from the National Trust car park at Langdon Hill, or approach from the villages to east and west along the coast. There is also a car park at Stonebarrow, with an information centre in an old radar station.

Greenhill Down

A small nature reserve which can be reached from the car park in Hilton village, near Milton Abbas. (Please do not obstruct the church.) Leave the car park and walk up the hill.

Hardy's Monument

Turn right at Portesham off the B3157 Weymouth/Bridport road.

The Portland stone tower commemorates the life of Admiral Sir Thomas Masterman Hardy, Nelson's Flag Captain on board HMS Victory at the Battle of Trafalgar. Admiral Hardy lived at nearby Portesham until he entered the Royal Navy. The tower is sited on Black Down, on the inland route of the Dorset Coast Path. There are views of Chesil and the Fleet, with much wider ranging views on clear days. The area is excellent for walking, with many waymarked paths.

Hardy's Monument, Black Down.

Holt Heath National Nature Reserve

Access is best from the Forestry Commission car park at White Sheet Hill, off the road from Holt to Three-Legged Cross.

Made a National Nature Reserve in 1985, Holt is one of the largest remaining lowland heaths in Dorset. Home to many unusual plants, birds and reptiles, the 1,500 acres are criss-crossed with tracks and paths.

Melbury Deer Park

Turn left off the Dorchester/Yeovil road to Evershot, and at the bottom of East Hill as you approach the village there are two linked turnings on the right, with a stone slab seat in the triangle. A walk up this road leads through the gate piers and into Melbury Deer Park.

The public right of way is the tarmac road through the park, so it is an ideal walk when the weather is wet underfoot. The parkland surrounding Melbury House is extensive, with glimpses of the house through the trees, on the far side of the lake. Dogs may be taken, but must be kept on a lead. The village of Evershot is also worthy of exploration: see Tess Cottage, next to the church, where Tess of the d'Urbervilles visited in Hardy's book.

Portland Sculpture Park

In Tout Quarry. There is free parking, turn left off the zig-zags by the Portland Heights Hotel. Walk back past the War Memorial, cross the road, and the quarry is ahead and to the left.

A good footpath affords an exhilarating walk around Portland's coast, with marvellous views of Chesil and the Fleet. The walk goes as far as Portland Bill for those with unlimited energy. Inside the quarry are many examples of sculpture in stone: unconventional, and not easy to find. The quarry itself is an unusual place to spend an afternoon. You can still see the tracks of the wagons which took the quarry spoil to the land edge, where it was tipped.

Powerstock Common

A3066 Bridport/Beaminster, turn right for Powerstock and continue beyond the village.

A small nature reserve of varied habitats, which includes a disused railway line. There is a car park. Dorset Trust for Nature Conservation run many of these small reserves in the county, but stress that although they enjoy public access they are intended primarily for people interested in conservation.

Radipole RSPB Reserve
In the centre of Weymouth. A Visitor Centre is situated beside the Swannery car park, and there are walks and hides around the lake.

Ringmoor
There is a car park at the Okeford Hill (north west of Blandford Forum) picnic site, and a footpath leads from here to Ringmoor. National Trust owned downland and woods, with good walking.

Stanpit Marsh
On the inner reaches of Christchurch harbour. These 150 acres were declared a nature reserve in 1967, and include about two thirds of the harbour wetlands. The chalk rivers of the Avon and Stour and biologically rich and this, combined with the fact that it lies on an important migration route, has made the area exceptionally good for the study of migratory and winter visiting birds. In 1986, Stanpit Marsh was declared a Site of Special Scientific Interest.

St Catherine's Hill
Two miles north west of Christchurch, off the road leading to Hurn.
   163' above sea level, this earthworks marks the site of the medieval chapel of St Catherine. It has been designated a Site of Special Scientific Interest because of its geology and the rare heathland wildlife it supports.
   There is a marked nature trail, and on a clear day it is possible to see the Isle of Wight from the viewpoint.

Stinsford/Bockhampton river walk
The churchyard at Stinsford, just east of Dorchester, is the resting place for Thomas Hardy's heart, buried in his first wife's grave. The banks of the nearby River Frome provide a walk back into Dorchester, and a lovely tree-lined walk past Kingston Maurward to Lower Bockhampton where Hardy went to school.

Hardy's Cottage, Thorncombe Woods

At Higher Bockhampton (0305-262366), 3 miles east of Dorchester off the A35. The cottage is 10 minutes walk from the car park.

The thatched cottage that was Thomas Hardy's home is now owned by the National Trust, and the exterior may be viewed from the end of the garden. The cottage is attractively sited, and many nearby paths make Thorncombe Woods easily explored and enjoyed. In June, nearby Rhododendron Mile makes a wonderful picnic spot and a beautiful photograph. There are also nature trails.

Tyneham

South east of the B3070 through West and East Lulworth.

The villagers of Tyneham, near Worbarrow Bay, moved out in 1943 when the Army took over the surrounding acres as a firing range. It was thought that they would return at the end of the war, but the Army has retained the land and the ruined village is a stark reminder of a once thriving community. There is a small museum in the Parish Church of St Mary – local and natural history, and archaeology.

Public access is usually at weekends and school holidays when the ranges are not in use: a car park next to the village, or parking on top of the ridge with a stiff but enjoyable walk down into the valley. An interesting Tyneham Trail is available from the Tourist Information Centre.

Wootton Hill

A forest walk, just north of the A35 Bridport/Lyme Regis road. There is a car park and picnic site. A narrow road turns off right at Morecombelake.

Winyard's Gap

Near Chedington, turn right, off the A356 Dorchester to Crewkerne road. A National Trust area with beautiful views. It was given in memory of the men of the 43rd Wessex Division who died in Normandy in 1944.

The cottage in which Thomas Hardy was born, Upper Bockhampton.

Country crafts are thriving, as more and more people appreciate the skills of yesteryear. Dorset's craftworkers can hold their own with the best, as can be seen not only at the following centres but in craft shows throughout the summer. Watch out for the traditional Dorset buttons – tight Catherine wheels of woven colour – and Dorset feather stitching on embroidered articles.

Alderholt Mill

Just off the B3078 between Alderholt and Sandleheath near Fordingbridge. Open Easter to end September, mid November to Christmas. Tues to Fri and Sun 2-6pm; Sat and Bank Hols, 10-6pm. Tel 0425-653130 for information.

A mill was recorded on the site in the 14th century and the present machinery worked regularly until 1942. The craft shop and art gallery (three-weekly exhibitions) were opened in 1982, the profits of which go to maintaining and restoring the machinery to full working order. Flour milling on Sundays. Own flour, biscuits and fudge for sale; ices, tea, coffee and soft drinks.

Broadwindsor

Broadwindsor (near Beaminster) Craft Centre is situated on the edge of the village on the Beaminster road. The craft centre, Gallery and restaurant make imaginative use of converted farm buildings, and there is a large car park.

Open every day including Sundays, 10am – 5pm, from 1 March to Christmas. Enquiries tel: 0308-68362.

The shops sell quality crafts and gifts made locally, as well as those from further afield. The Gallery mounts a frequently changing exhibition of the work of local artists and craftsmen.

Courtyard Centre

3.5 miles from Poole, in Huntick Road, Lytchett Minster. To the rear of South Lytchett Manor Caravan Park and off the Dorchester Road between Upton and the Baker's Arms roundabout. Well signposted.

Open daily 10am – 5pm except Mondays. Closed during Christmas week. Open all other Bank Holidays. Car park. Tel: 0202-623423 for information – Mike or Linda Wise.

A converted Georgian farm complex surrounding a large paved courtyard houses this arts and crafts centre, which includes working crafts, a tile pottery, childrens' pets corner and garden centre; also a country food restaurant with licensed bar, barn for functions, and a recording studio! There is a display of early farm and country bygones.

Poole Pottery

On Poole Quay. Showroom shop and tearoom open all year round including Bank Holidays, 10 – 5pm. Closed Christmas week. Open evenings and Sundays in summer.

Crafts Centre and Museum open March to Christmas Eve, including Bank Hols, 10am – 4.30pm every day. Last admissions 4pm. Tel: 0202-668681 for information.

The centre includes an exhibition of pottery making over the years, a gallery where potters can be seen at work, painting studio, and a glass-blowing hall where this fascinating craft is demonstrated. Other Dorset local crafts are also on view, together with static displays, models and videos. Entry to all areas is free.

Walford Mill

Stone Lane, off B3078, just north of Wimborne Minster Town Centre. The restored 18th century building, sited on an island in the River Allen, may be reached by a riverside walk from Wimborne main car park. Open every day 10am – 5pm (except Mons January – 31 March, Christmas and New Year's day). Tel: 0202-841400 for information.

Home of the Dorset Craft Guild since 1986, the complex contains a quality crafts shop, exhibition gallery, workshop area and a licensed restaurant in an attractive riverside setting. Entrance and car parking are free, but occasionally a small charge is made for a particular exhibition.

Worth Farm Craft Centre and Museum

In the village of Worth Matravers, the heart of Purbeck. This centre was established in 1990, and is expanding. There are craft workshops plus shop, and tea rooms. There is a museum, too, with a small entry charge.

As part of the Countryside Stewardship Scheme a footpath now runs across the historic lynchetts nearby to link with the Dorset Coast Path, and there are 60 acres of land open to public access. Telephone Mr David Strange for more information, 0929 439210

Walford Mill, Wimborne Minster.

EDIBLE DORSET

Dorset Knobs, Blue Vinney cheese and a bottle of Hardy ale - a picnic fit for a king! But why not investigate oysters? Or the excellent hams and ice-cream of Denhay and Childhay? The following welcome visitors, and hope you will develop a taste for Dorset.

Abbotsbury Oysters

At Ferrybridge, Weymouth. Open 7 days a week, 'phone Weymouth 788867 for information.

Abbotsbury oysters are grown in the Fleet behind Chesil Bank. The Fleet lagoon has been a reserve ever since the 11th century, and is been maintained by the Fox-Strangways family. The Nature Conservancy Council now has a hand in ensuring the waters remain pure.

One million oysters a year are grown, taking 2 years to reach a ready-to-eat size. Oysters can be bought direct, sampled straight from the water, and can be sent as a gift. Visitors are welcome to look round this fascinating venture.

Childhay Manor

In conjunction with the National Farmers Union there are farms in Dorset which open to the public several times a year. Open Days are advertised locally and in the press, and enquiries may be made through the NFU office in Beaminster (tel: 0308-862774).

Childhay Manor, Blackdown, Beaminster, is a working farm with two dairies; an outdoor pig breeding herd and pig fattening unit; a flock of sheep; and cream and ice-cream manufacturing.

Farm open days show visitors all these aspects and how they integrate. Childhay West Country Dairy Ice Cream has become so popular that in 1992 this part of the business will be moving to a new location in Crewkerne, just over the Somerset border. It is hoped that the Crewkerne site, too, will give visitors the chance to see Childhay Manor farming at work.

Denhay Farm, Bridport

Denhay Farm, situated in the beautiful Marshwood Vale, holds two
or three open days a year. Visitors are shown the cheesehouse and
given a brief tour of the farm. There is also a nature trail of about
1 mile. The Marshwood Vale is an Area of Outstanding Natural
Beauty, and wildlife and conservation play a key part in running the
farm.

Denhay make prize-winning Cheddar cheese, and are also renown
for specially cured ham. There is a Farm Shop open on Mondays and
Thursdays.

Moores Biscuit Bakery

On the south side of the A35 in Morecombelake, 4 miles west of
Bridport. The bakery is open Monday – Friday, 9am to 5pm,
throughout the year.

Moores Dorset Biscuits began with the making of Dorset Knobs in
1850 at Stoke Mills, in the Marshwood Vale. Dorset Knobs were a
traditional meal for local farm workers at the start of the day. In about
1880 the bakery at Morecombelake was opened, and is the only part
of the family business surviving today.

As well as Dorset Knobs, the bakery now produces a fine range of
sweet biscuits. There is a small art gallery on the premises, and a
shop selling not just the Moores biscuits but also many other West
Country products.

EVENTS

Coast and country combine in a backdrop for a wonderful variety of events. Fireworks come to the fore in carnivals, and especially in the spectacular displays of the Weymouth International Firework Festival. Village street fairs take a step back in time, while Bournemouth International Airport looks to the future with its Air Show. Many more events are planned each year. Tourist Information Offices will be right up to date, and local papers can be checked for last minute details.

Beaminster
Point-to-point races at Toller Down Gate – March/April.
Town fair – May.

Bournemouth
Bristol/Bournemouth Vintage Vehicle Run – June.
Festival of Flowers – June.
International Airport (Hurn) air show – August.
Regatta and Carnival – first week in August.
Kids Free and Fun Festival – August.
Festival of Lights – end of August.

Bridport
Carnival – mid August.
Torchlight procession – Sunday following Carnival.
West Bay Day – August Bank Holiday Sunday.

Buckland Newton
Goose Auction – late May Bank Holiday.

Christchurch
Carnival and regatta – mid August, with a fair on the Quay on the Saturday, followed by fireworks. Sunday procession.

Corfe Castle

Ancient Order of Marblers and Stonecutters meeting – Shrove Tuesday. One pound of peppercorn is taken through the streets of Corfe, from the Fox Inn to Ower Quay where stone used to be shipped out of Purbeck.

Carnival – August.

Dorchester

Carnival – June.

Sheep Fair – October.

Lyme Regis

Regatta and Carnival – first week in August.

Milton Abbas

Street Fair – biannually, odd years, July.

Mudeford

Trawler Race – July/August.

Poole

Bath Tub Race – New Year's Day.

Dawn celebration of May Day – 1st May.

Fishermans' Regatta – July.

RNLI Open Day - beginning of August. Tel: 0202-671133 for information, as lifeboats can be visited in several locations at this time.

Needles Trophy International Power Boat Race – third week in August.

Arts Centre – frequent free exhibitions tel: 0202-670521.

Portland

Island Fling – late May/early June.

Carnival – end of July.

Puddletown

Carnival – July.

Shaftesbury
Gold Hill Fair — end of September.

Sherborne
Carnival — August.
Pack Monday Fair — first Monday after the 10th October.

Swanage
Carnival and regatta — first week in August, beginning and ending
with fireworks.
Water Sports Festival — last week in May.
Oudoor band concerts - usually Sundays at 3pm and 7pm at the
Bandstand, Recreation Ground.

Tolpuddle
Martyrs Trades Union Rally — 3rd Sunday in July.

Wareham
Carnival — July.

Weymouth
This seaside town provides the most amazing variety of spectator
events from February to November. Listed are the major events,
many of which are annual and free:
March:
Sailing Regatta
Hockey Festival
Squash Festival
April:
National Powerboat Racing
Water Ski selection races
Squash championships
May:
Windsurfing Championships
International Kite Festival
Water Regatta and Trawler Race
Kite Festival
Dorset Tour Car Rally

Vintage Motor Cycle Rally
Oyster Festival
Tennis Tournament
June:
Tall Ship visit
RAF Town Show
Sailing selection trials
July:
Tennis tournament
International Firework Festivals
Sailing Regatta
Bowls Tournament
Sailing Championships
Tall Ship visit
August:
Radio 1 Roadshow
Beach Volleyball
International Firework Festivals
Bowls Tournament
Windsurfing Championships
Carnival and fireworks – the third Wednesday in August.
September:
Vintage & Classic Car Rally
Tennis Tournament
October:
Beach Moto-Cross
November:
5th – beach bonfire and fireworks

Wimborne
Point-to-point races at Badbury Rings – March/April.
Folk Festival – early June.

HISTORIC BUILDINGS

For lovers of church architecture, probably every village church in Dorset is worth a visit. The county also boasts four major abbeys. Included in this secton are other buildings of historic interest, but of course there are many more. Some, like Horton Tower and Creech Folly, are interesting viewed from a distance, their contribution to the skyline being of more importance than an interior. Lulworth and Sandsfoot castles are interesting ruins.

Bere Regis Church

One of the most visited parish churches in Dorset, with its beautiful timbered roof. The lovely exterior stonework and elegant tower make this an eye-catching example of church architecture, but the interior is even more remarkable — extensively carved and decorated in exuberant fashion.

It is believed the roof was financed by Cardinal John Morton, an Archbishop of Canterbury. He was born in Bere Regis, and on his death left money to the church. This building makes a fascinating comparison with the rustic church of Winterborne Tomson, just up the road.

Christchurch Priory

Open daily throughout the year, 9.30 am to 5.30 pm. Sundays 2.15 pm to 5.30 pm. There are often free organ recitals on Thursday lunchtimes, telephone the Head Verger (0202-485804) for information. Adjacent municipal car park.

This beautiful building was started in 1094 by Ralph Flambard, Chief Minister of King William II, although there has been a church here since Saxon times.

The original site chosen for a place of worship was on St Catherine's Hill, north of the present town. It is said that building materials which were assembled during the day were mysteriously removed at night to the present site, close to where the rivers meet.

Believing this to be a sign of God's will, the site was changed.

The Priory encompasses a wide range of architectural styles, and is the longest parish church in England, at 311 feet 9 inches.

The Priory is famous for the legend of the Miraculous Beam. During construction a huge beam was prepared and hoisted into position, and then was found to have been cut too short. Next morning the worried builders were amazed to find the beam had been 'miraculously' lengthened, to fit its intended space. They recalled then that the carpenters had had an extra man in their team for whom no-one could vouch. They believed he must have been the Carpenter of Nazareth, and the church was named after Him – Christ Church.

Dorchester Crown Court

Open Monday to Friday (May to October), 9am to 1pm, 2pm – 4pm; Monday to Friday, (November to April), 10am to mid-day. Enquiries 0305-251010.

Situated in High West Street, entry is through the District Council Offices. In this late 18th century court, six farm workers from

The Old Crown Court, Dorchester.

Tolpuddle were sentenced in 1834 to seven years transportation for forming 'The Friendly Society of Agricultural Labourers', forerunner of the Trades Union Movement.

Dorchester, Roman Town House

In Colliton Park, behind County Hall, are the remains of a Roman town house. One mosaic is on view, others having been moved to the County Museum. Nearby West Walks, on the line of the old Roman walls, link with South Walks and the River Frome path to provide a pleasant route around the outskirts of town. The only remaining piece of Roman wall can be seen just south of Top o' Town roundabout.

Lulworth Castle

Situated at East Lulworth, this derelict castle was designed by Inigo Jones. It was built in the early 17th century as a mansion house, in medieval castle style, but was gutted by fire in 1929. It is now being restored by English Heritage, to be completed by 1993. There is public footpath access off the East Lulworth road, through a white gate signposted 'St Andrew's Church'.

Milton Abbey

The Abbey Church is open all the year round during daylight hours. Entrance is free, except over the Easter week-end and during school summer holidays when parts of the Mansion House are also open to the public, usually with an exhibition which may be visited at the same time. A charge is then made which covers entrance to grounds, Mansion, and Abbey. Donations are welcome.

The entrance through the west door, with its wonderful views across the Dorset countryside, leads into the fan-vaulted Crossing. There is an annual music festival here, taking advantage of the superb acoustics.

The favourite story surrounding the Abbey Church is of John Tregonwell who, as a child, fell from the roof. His stiff skirts belled out like a parachute, slowing his fall, and he landed unharmed. In his Will he left a small library of books to the abbey, but only one remains of this collection today.

Sited in the lovely Delcombe valley, the church is adjacent to the

Mansion House which is now a public school for boys. It is about one mile from Milton Abbas, and may be approached by public footpath from that village, or by car into the grounds of the school.

The church was rebuilt in its present form between the 13th and 15th centuries, on the site of a monastery founded by King Athelstan.

Both church and monastery passed into private hands in 1529, and in the 18th century the surrounding village of Middleton (later shortened to Milton) was destroyed by the landlord, the Earl of Dorchester, and Milton Abbas as it is seen today was built. The only surviving houses of Middleton are Dale Cottage beyond the lake, and the cottage by the grass steps, Green Walk Cottage.

Moreton Church

Of all Dorset's small churches, this is an unexpected treasure. 'Lawrence of Arabia' is buried nearby.

In 1940 a bomb destroyed all the windows in the church, and these have gradually been replaced with clear glass engraved by Lawrence Whistler.

The designs are intricate and beautiful, and give a wonderful overall effect. The theme is 'light' — most appropriate when the sunlight streams in and enhances the delicate engravings.

Sandsfoot Castle, Weymouth

Sandsfoot Castle was one of a chain of coastal forts built in the time of Henry VIII. Together with Portland Castle immediately opposite, Sandsfoot stood guard over this important harbour.

Pieces of 12th century stonework found in parts of the Castle fallen to the beach are believed to have come from Bindon Abbey, which was reduced to ruin in 1539. Sandsfoot was built in 1541. The chain continues, with stone from the ruined Sandsfoot being used in other Weymouth buildings, including the Town Bridge.

Little remains today. The ruin is small but impressive, in a beautiful position. Seats, formal garden and pond complete the approach from Old Castle Road.

Sherborne Abbey

The Abbey was founded in 705 AD by the Saxon Saint Adhelm as his cathedral, but gradually fell into disrepair. Early in the 15th century rebuilding work was begun, and included the glorious fan vaulting for which the church is famed.

It became the abbey church of the adjoining Benedictine monastery, and at the Dissolution the townspeople raised the money to buy the abbey. It has been Sherborne's parish church ever since.

The bell chamber contains the heaviest peal of eight bells in the world, the tenor alone weighs 46 cwt (2.3 tonnes). On New Year's Eve the Abbey clock strikes 13 at midnight, and the New Year is rung in.

St Catherine's Chapel, Abbotsbury

High on a hill overlooking village and coast, this 14th century chapel is thought to have originally been a sea chapel. It makes an excellent landmark for sailors.

Legend has it that a spinster's prayer offered to St Catherine ensured her a husband. After the stiff climb up the hill, one hopes she was not too disappointed!

Wimborne Minster

Open daily 9 – 5.30 pm. The Minster was built on the site of an 8th century monastery. It is a cruciform building, constructed of two contrasting types of stone, one grey, one brown, which give an unusual chequerboard appearance. It is one of the great churches and historic landmarks of southern England, its twin towers dominating the town. The various architectural styles encompass 1000 years of history.

The Western Tower is 95 feet high, and has a peal of 10 bells. On the north side of the tower the Quarter Jack strikes the bells either side at every quarter-hour. This wooden figure is dressed as a grenadier of the British Army at the time of the Napoleonic wars.

Look out for the 14th century astronomical clock, one of the earliest in the country, and the rare three-sided sundial. A Saxon chest on display is hewn from a single log.

Winterborne Tomson Church

Off the A31 Bere Regis/Wimborne road, turn left signposted Anderson.

The interior of this tiny church has been likened to an upturned boat, a description of the rib-like roof timbering. The pews, pulpit and gallery date from around 1720, and were restored in 1930. It is a building of simple charm.

Woolbridge Manor, Wool.

MARKETS AND SHOPS

All the major towns in the county have good shopping. In particular the Bournemouth arcades are full of interesting boutiques, while the town centre boasts many of the larger modern stores. The indoor Dolphin Centre at Poole has a wide range of shops all under one roof, and the speciality units in the 'period' shopping village of Brewers' Quay at Weymouth are proving a popular attraction.

The latter is a restored old brewery in the heart of the harbour area, and includes seasonal festivities and fun events for all the family which are widely advertised. It is open from 10am – 6pm in winter, 10am – 10pm in summer.

There are also markets. Most towns have a small weekly market, some better known than others. Three are particularly good:

Dorchester
The county town has its main market on Wednesdays, the site being opposite Dorchester South Station. There are several hundred stalls, and the market includes an antiques and bric-a-brac covered area. Starting early, the market begins to close just after lunch – depending on trade. The first and third Thursdays in the month the site is used as a cattle market.

Since the market site is used for car parking on non-market days, the loss of these spaces mean that to park anywhere near the town centre an early start is advisable.

Sturminster Newton
In the north of the county, Sturminster Newton – 'Stur' as it is known locally – is famous for its cattle market. This is held on Mondays, when the town becomes devoted to farmers and farming.

Sturminster Newton has a very small shopping centre, but it includes some interesting antique shops and small streets worth exploring.

Wimborne Minster

One of the largest open and covered markets in the south of England. It is well signposted throughout the area, and there is plenty of free parking. Wilts & Dorset run a special bus service on Fridays and Sundays, 'phone 0202-673555 for details.

The Friday market operates from 7am until 2.30pm and includes the famous Antiques and Bric-a-Brac Bazaar. Saturday Flea Markets operate from 9am until approximately 1pm. The larger Sunday Market operates from 10am until 4pm.

Other market days:

Blandford — Thursday/Saturday
Bridport — Wednesday/Saturday
Christchurch — Monday
Poole — Saturday
Shaftesbury — Thursday
Sherborne — Thursday/Saturday
Wareham — Thursday
Weymouth — Thursday (Monday — summer only)

MUSEUMS

There are many, and varied, museums in the county. None are expensive to visit – often justs a few pence. However the following are free, and cover a wide range of interests as well as offering a fascinating insight into the history of Dorset.

Corfe Castle
West Street, Corfe Castle. This tiny village museum is on the ground floor of the Town Hall, believed to be the smallest Town Hall building in the country. It is open daily from April to October, 9am – 5pm.

Displays of local bygones, early implements from nearby clay workings, and dinosaur footprints.

Gillingham
Church Walk, Gillingham, just west of St Mary's Church. Open April to September, Wednesdays 2.30pm – 4.30pm, Saturdays 10.30am – 4.30pm. Tel: 0747-822810/823176.

Gillingham local history, relating to 'the ancient Royal Manor, the Forest and Royal Peculiar'. There are 13th and 14th century documents and exhibits, and a small fossil display.

Mill House Cider
A352 or B3390 6 miles south east of Dorchester. Halfway between Owermoigne and Crossways. Open every day 9-1 and 2-5pm. (Closed 4 days over Christmas, and New Year's Day.) Tel: 0305-852220.

18th and 19th century cider making equipment including mills and presses is displayed in the museum, and is used between October and December. A video shows the story of traditional farm cider when the presses are not in use, between January and September.

Net Manufacture

Bridgeacre, Uploders, Bridport. Open 2.30pm – 5.30pm (except May and September), and by appointment with Bridport Museum. Tel: 0308-22116. (Bridport Museum is itself open free of charge on Sundays.)

There are special exhibitions which change from time to time, but the museum basically is an international collection relating to all aspects of net manufacture.

Royal National Lifeboat Institution

West Quay Road, Poole. A small museum open 9am – 5pm weekdays all year. Not Bank Holidays. Tel: 0202-671133.

There is also an old lifeboat on display in Old Lifeboat House, East Quay, Poole, which is open 10.30am – 5pm Easter weekend, Whit weekend, then every day until the end of September.

Royal Signals Regiment

Blandford Camp, well signposted off the Blandford Forum bypass. Open 10am – 5pm Monday to Friday from June to September. Weekends and holiday periods, 10am – 4pm. Tel: 0258-452581 to confirm arrangements.

Items dealing with the history of Army communications from the Crimean War to the Falkland Islands campaign; also uniforms, badges, medals, vehicles including military motorcycles, and the only example of the horse drawn cable laying wagon.

Shelley Rooms

Shelley Park, Bournemouth. Tel: 0202-303571. In a part of Boscombe Manor which was once the home of Shelley's son, Percy Florence Shelley. Open Monday to Saturday, 2pm – 5pm.

The poet Shelley's life and work are displayed. There is also a small library covering this subject which visitors are welcome to use.

Southern Electric

Old Generating Station, Bargates, Christchurch. Open 10-4pm Monday, Wednesday and Friday, 1 March to end September. Tel: 0202-480467.

An extensive collection of historic electrical equipment. More than 700 exhibits from large steam and water driven generators to old domestic equipment, including hands-on working models. Something to fascinate everyone; housed in a building dating from 1903.

Tolpuddle Martyrs
A 35, Tolpuddle, near Dorchester. Open dawn to dusk. Tel: 0305-848237.

The museum and six cottages were built by the Trades Union Congress in 1934. They commemorate the six Tolpuddle Martyrs who endured transportation to Australia in 1834 after forming the first Trades Union. Exhibits include photographs and documents. (See Dorchester Old Crown Court under Historic Buildings.)

Wareham
East Street, Wareham. Open Monday to Saturday from Easter to mid October 10am – 1pm and 2pm – 5pm. Manned by volunteers, tel: 0929-553448 to confirm opening.

Displays of local bygones including agricultural implements, information on Old Wareham, and a special section on Lawrence of Arabia.

PARKS AND GARDENS

There are usually Borough Gardens to be found in the towns, a quiet spot for adults to relax, and sometimes with play areas for the children. The following are on a larger scale.

Bournemouth Central Gardens

In Bournemouth's town centre, Central Gardens sweep back either side of the Bourne Stream. Many mature trees and shrubs provide shade and seclusion, and an ideal background for the summer displays of colourful bedding plants.

The area nearest the beach is called Lower Gardens, and regular bandstand concerts are held here during the summer season. Central and Upper Gardens are quieter, the stream overhung with weeping willows and paths bordered by flowering shrubs.

Poole Park

Set on the edge of Poole Harbour, one minute's walk from the Town Centre, the park is open throughout the year. The car park is free, but is only available after 10am.

One hundred acres of parkland, gardens and lakes mean overcrowding is rare. Opened at the end of the 19th century, it has remained a popular recreational venue. Local events throughout the year make full use of the park, including the start of the Poole Marathon which is enjoyed by large numbers of spectators.

Weymouth Nothe Gardens

There is car parking by the gardens which are well signposted from Weymouth centre, but it is more pleasant to park near Hope Square and follow the harbourside walk. This way you will enjoy the Wedding Cascade opened to commemorate the marriage of the Prince of Wales to Lady Diana.

Steps lead up from the walk past Nothe Fort and on to the gardens. There are no colourful formal flower beds. Shrub borders and trees line the walks, and shade the grassy spaces where there are plenty of seats. The gardens are set on a headland, with magnificent views over Weymouth Bay and Esplanade to the north, and Portland Harbour to the south.

There is a barbecue, and several level terraces where picnics can be enjoyed. A public footpath leads from the gardens over the next small headland and past the coastguard station, taking in the shore line, Castle Cove, along Underbarn Walk to Sandsfoot Castle.

TOWN TRAILS

Beaminster

The town stands at the head of the valley of the River Brit where many tributaries join together, and the streets tend to follow the line of the streams which in earlier times flowed above ground in many parts. The earliest recorded version (possibly 7th century) of the name Beaminster is Bebingmynster, and the most likely meaning is Church of Bebbe, this being a female personal name. No trace has so far been found, however, of the early minster church; the existing church, St Mary's, is basically 15th century with a little 13th century work.

A charter was granted in 1284 for a weekly market all day Thursday and a three-day annual fair in September, and by the end of medieval times the agricultural settlement had certainly grown into a little town, with a stepped cross in the centre of its market-place. Prosperity came through the manufacture of wool cloth and in the 17th century there was a fine market house on stone arched pillars.

Hemp and flax manufacturers also developed – sailcloth, sackcloth, shoe-thread, rope and twine. Many other small industries were carried on, for example paper-making, printing, potteries and metal-working, but the buildings have since been pulled down or adapted for different uses.

Strongly Parliamentarian, the town was devastated in 1644 in a fire started by the occupying Royalist army; in 1684 the centre was severely burnt through an accidental fire. The finest 17th century houses are to be found on the fringe of the town where they escaped the fires. A further fire in 1781 affected Church Street, Hogshill Street and Shadrack Street, and the centre of Beaminster today has a largely late 18th century and early 19th century appearance.

The population declined after 1841 when the industries failed, the railway did not come near the town, and the flight from the land led to a great fall in numbers employed in agriculture. Growth has taken place since the last war and the population today is 2,800. The town

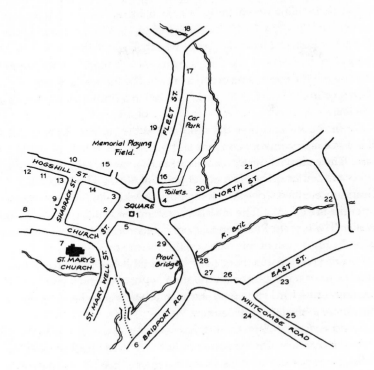

has an excellent range of shops and numerous thriving societies; it has become a favourite with retired people.

The centre of Beaminster is a Conservation Area and contains over 200 Listed buildings. The walk takes just over an hour. Three short extensions are shown in italics and to do all of these you will need an extra 20 – 30 minutes.

The trail starts in The Square at the Robinson Memorial (1), locally known as 'Julia' because it was erected by Vincent Robinson of Parnham in memory of his sister in 1906. In the style of a covered market cross, the building is of Ham stone, but the pinnacles of Portland stone were brought from the demolished Christ's Hospital in London. Going round The Square clockwise, the attractive Italianate building occupied by Lloyd's Bank (2) was erected for an earlier bank in 1872. Note the variety of capitals to the ground floor window pilasters, including ears of wheat. The building now Pickwicks Inn (3) was once the King's Arms and the most important inn in the town – the name is recorded in 1619. The inn was severely damaged in the fire of 1781 which started in a tinsmith's workshop at the rear.

On the opposite corner, the shopfront at the entrance to Fore Place has some nice ironwork columns and tracery. The facade of the Midland Bank, a town house of some distinction, was refashioned in the mid 18th century. The Fleet Street gable of No 12 The Square (4) bears an inscribed stone which records the rebuilding of the house after the fire of 1684. The initials W L stand for William Lacke, a cloth maker. The present Red Lion was only constructed in 1892, but there was already an inn of this name on the site in 1618.

Frampton & Son, butchers, have been established in the town for about 140 years. A plaque on the shop (5) just beyond commemorates Richard Hine who started a grocer's and chemist's business there in the late 18th century.

Go down Church Street which has several pleasant cottages, mostly later 18th century. On the corner of St Mary Well Street is the Eight Bells, formerly the Five Bells; it was renamed when the number of bells in the church tower was increased in 1765.

If you have time, take a stroll along St Mary Well Street, known in the early 19th century as Duck Street – the stream under the roadway then ran above ground between cobbled paths skirting the cottages. Leave the street and follow the path beside the now open stream to the weir at Hams, where it joins the River Brit. Nearby there used to be a corn mill, probably on the same site as one of the mills mentioned in the Domesday Book. At one time, water in the tail race of a paper mill in the Bridport road ran back into the river here. Between 1754 and 1881, tolls were taken at the turnpike gates which spanned the road to Bridport at South Gate (6); the last house on the right incorporates the chimney of the old turnpike house.

The walk continues up the slope through the churchyard. Do visit the church: it is outside the scope of this walk but you will find a special guide and some informative notices set up around. The Tower (7), built about 1500, is 100 feet high, which is unusual for Dorset; it has fine figure sculpture on the west face including Crucifixion, Resurrection and Ascension, and what are thought to be two donors.

At the far end of the churchyard, an inscription on the south side of a little one-storey Ham stone building tells us that it was endowed by Sir John Strode (of Parnham House, on the way to Bridport) in 1630. It served as an almshouse for up to six poor people for nearly 350 years and was restored for use as a meeting-room to commemorate the Silver Jubilee of Queen Elizabeth II in 1977. Go down the steps. Just along Shorts Lane the late 18th century Minster House (8) has a fine brick facade with a decorative band of four courses of alternating burnt header bricks.

Retracing your way, turn up Shadrack Street – the origin of the name is Shittrick, meaning dung ditch. The passage on the left once led into a yard where leather used to be tanned. In 1832 a gasometer was set up there to supply gas to the town, one of the earliest of such ventures outside London. Between 1843 and 1868 a private school for boys, known as Beaminster Classical and Commercial Academy, was held in Shadrack House (9); the schoolroom was the extension on the right. The round brick chimney on the last building at the top of the street (right) shows that it was once a baker's premises. Look across at the imposing London House (10) dominating Hogshill Street with its tall chimneys; the house was built in 1862 for the Coombs family who had a large drapery business and a printing press there.

A diversion along Hogshill Street to your left takes you to see two more 19th century school buildings. The Girls and Infants Elementary School (11), with teacher's house behind, now dwellings, was built in 1868; before that the National School, which had been opened in 1830, was held in part of the old parish workhouse. Hamilton Lodge opposite is on the site of a factory owned by wool-cloth manufacturer John Hamilton. A little farther along, the premises of the former Beaminster and Netherbury Grammar School (12) were erected in 1897 on the site of the 18th century potteries where coarse ware and agricultural drainage pipes had been made.

Cross Hogshill Street and look back at the building with large portico of Greek Doric columns on the corner of Shadrack Street, now known as Daniels House (13). It was to his family home on this site that James Daniel, a nonconformist attorney, returned after his escape from the Battle of Sedgemoor (1685), at which he fought for the

Duke of Monmouth. A brick rear wing in Shadrack Street survives from the early 18th century, but the main part of the house was virtually burnt down in the fire of 1781 and rebuilt.

A number of properties between here and The Square were also destroyed. No 19 Hogshill Street (14), built in 1783, has a fine ashlar stone front with two rows of four sash windows but, strangely, no door; if the gate happens to be open, there is a lovely view of the church tower across the garden. The premises of Francis Bugler Ltd, agricultural engineers, were formerly the New Inn; the firm was established elsewhere in the town about 1850.

Continue along Hogshill Street to the large town house Champions (15), now premises of Kitson & Trotman, solicitors. It has a typically 19th century facade, but go up the passage towards the Memorial Playing Field and you will find mullion windows at the back; the house was built about 1700. The White Hart next door is mid 19th century, but an inn here with this name was already one of Beaminster's main hostelries in the 17th century.

Turning into Fleet Street, note the attractive building formerly Pines Ltd, Grocers, with its two bow windows and continuous cornice over windows and doorway. Almost opposite is the archway of the former Swan Inn. Since the inn was closed in 1935 and converted, the building has been used for a number of offices and services: first Town Offices, then NFS Fire Station in the Second World War, Beaminster Rural District Council Offices (1947-74) and now again Town Council Offices and Library.

The Public Hall (16), built by voluntary subscriptions and opened in 1903, stands on part of the site of a large sailcloth factory run by the Cox family for a hundred years; the name 'Yarn Barton' refers to the enclosure for bleaching yarn which once extended up behind Fleet Street to the house named Barton End.

The last optional extension takes you up Fleet Street. Barton End (17) is well worth seeing. The stylish front range was added about 1730 at right angles to a 17th century stone house with mullioned windows. The symmetrical brick facade has a stone plinth and cornice and there are stone surrounds to the doorway and the five sash windows.

At the top of the street Abbot Brown, printers and engravers, employ a substantial work force. Here in the 17th century at 'Towns End' were corn and fulling mills. Opposite is Holy Trinity Church (18), opened in 1851 to serve what was seen as a growing population in the outlying hamlets and farms to the north; in actual fact the population of the parish as a whole had already begun to fall from its peak of 1841 (3270). The church is now a private residence. Next door is St John's Catholic Church, established in 1966. On your way back you will see on the right another closed and converted church, the Wesleyan Methodist Centenary Chapel (19), built in 1839.

A little way along North Street is No 15, The Red House (20), a pleasing early 18th century building best viewed from the opposite side of the road. The brick-fronted house has an unusual stone doorway with scrolled decoration; the surround of the central window above the door has shaped side pieces carved with open flowers. The mullions of the windows are interesting because they are flat-sectioned, the final style before mullions went out of fashion. The factory behind you (Aplin and Barrett), which now makes food preservatives, was set up in 1904 to produce Cow and Gate Dried Milk Powder. Earlier still there were workshops belonging to the enterprising Coombs family, makers of some of the first threshing machines about 1800.

Continuing up North Street, note the Tudor style doorway at No 19, and the two-storied canted bay window at No 21, among the few buildings near the town centre to survive the two great 17th century fires. Beaminster Manor (21) is a large square house erected in the late 18th century and remodelled in the early 19th. The fine iron gates have the initials M and C intertwined and were made for the lady of the manor, Mary Cox, by a local craftsman, William B Newman, around 1900. The stables, which have windows with architraves and pediments, were built about 1670.

Woodswater Lane makes a convenient link between North Street and East Street. The River Brit is crossed at a picturesque ford and footbridge (22). East Street still has something of a cottagey atmosphere at its farther end where most of the houses, some with door hoods, date to around 1800. The former Boys Elementary School (23), now residential, was opened in 1875, following on the first Elementary Education Act. It replaced the old parish workhouse, which housed poor people for over two hundred years.

We are now nearing the final stage of our walkabout, but with a cluster of splendid 17th century houses still to come. Be careful as you turn up Whitcombe Road because there are no footways. On the right Hitts House (24) is late 17th century. The central doorway has a delightful carved scallop-shell hood and the square 18th century gate piers are topped by balls. Farther along on the left the slightly earlier Edgeley Cottage (25) has a continuous dripstone, to throw off rain-water, over ground floor windows. By contrast, Wynford next door shows fine brick voussoirs over the windows.

Farrs (26) is notable for its tall yew hedge. The house consists of a rear block at right-angles to the street, to which was added early in the 18th century a symmetrical front range. The little gate in the wall has romantic associations with two prominent local families: in 1790 the heiress Ann Symes eloped from here to Gretna Green with Samuel Cox. The Congregational Chapel (27), according to an inscription on the south wall, was built in 1749 and enlarged in 1825. Earlier the Presbyterians, as·they were then known, met in a house nearby.

Until the late 18th century, Prout Bridge, where the road crosses the River Brit, was narrow and had steps; it could only be used by people on foot, horsemen and carriages having to splash through the ford. The facade of Bridge House (28) is early 17th century and not symmetrical, the doorway being off centre. An important house, it was occupied for 150 years by a series of doctors. The blue lias stone setts in front were probably laid down by the turnpike trust to provide a dry footway for travellers. On your left as you return to The Square is the former police station and magistrate's court, only closed in 1963. The Walnuts (29), next door but one, has an interesting facade dating to about 1820, with flat pilasters at either end.

Blandford Forum

There are now car parks at each end of the Conservation Area, one at the Ham, beside the bridge over the Stour, and the other at the east end of East Street, behind the Bere Regis 'bus station. In consequence, the route of this trail can be followed either clockwise or anti-clockwise, but the points of interest have been set out for a clockwise walk.

Park in the Marsh car park (1), call in at the Tourist Information Centre (2), and walk to the centre of the bridge over the Stour (3). The meadows on the left as you face the town were once the park of Bryanston House, now a public school, so no development took place

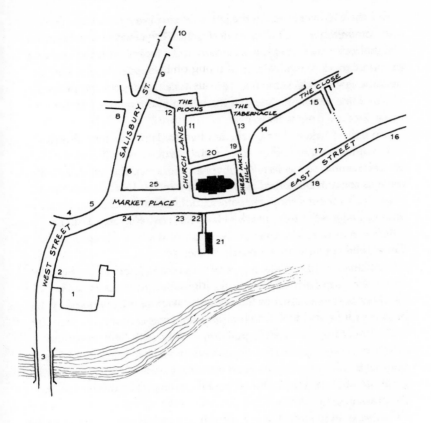

in that part of the town.

Notice the warning on the eastern parapet of the bridge, a warning echoed on many other bridges in Dorset. The Victorian lamp standard opposite was restored at the initiation of the Civic Society for the Queen's Silver Jubilee in 1978.

Blandford bridge is reputed to have its own ghost — that of a black dog — dating perhaps from the days when a dog was sacrificed beneath a road or a bridge to ensure safe passage.

There are two concrete pillboxes overlooking the meadows, built in the Second World War to protect the town. A milestone near the Crown Hotel gives the distance to Shaston (as Shaftesbury was then called).

Past the Crown Hotel, on the left, is No 10 West Street (4). This was completely rebuilt after its destruction by a lorry, but retains the original keystones over the windows, and a facade with the appropriate modern equivalents of the original 'header' bricks. This building leads on to some fine 18th century facades (5) and gives the visitor a fine panoramic view of the whole of the unique Market Place, looking from west to east.

Leave the Market Place by the left hand side of Salisbury Street. The buildings on the other side — from Durdens, with its coved plaster awning, to modern Woolworths higher up the hill — illustrate the evolution of Blandford as a market town. Mr Durden was the owner of a grocer's shop. He paid schoolchildren to collect Roman and Iron Age relics from nearby Hod Hill (now National Trust), which had been turned over as the result of wartime ploughing. These relics are now in the British Museum.

Mathematical tiling (a facing of tiles to resemble brick) can be seen above the shop with bow windows (6), and part of Cherry's. The gateway of the old Anchor Inn under its original oriel window (7) has brackets for fire ladders, which disappeared this century.

The Pork Shop (8) near the junction of Whitecliff Mill Street and Salisbury Street, has existed since the date on its fascia, though the original building must have been one of the earliest casualties of the great fire of 1731, which stared in a tallow-chandlers on the site of the present King's Arms.

Continue up the left side of Salisbury Street and note the inscription over the cycle shop, No 38, on the opposite side (9). Alfred Stevens became a well known and versatile artist, whose most famous work was a memorial to the Duke of Wellington, housed in St Paul's Cathedral. The Gallery on the ground floor of the Museum is named after him, and is used for exhibitions of local arts, crafts and lectures. Further up, on the same side of Salisbury Street, are the Ryves Almshouses (10). Built in 1682, before the last disastrous fire of 1731, these Houses gave accommodation to 10 impecunious persons, who paid 2/6d per week and were each presented with a grey gown. The Charity still provides shelter for five elderly people.

Return to the fork in the road and turn left into the Plocks, once an enclosure for sheep being kept in readiness for sale at market. Coupar House (11) at the top of Church Lane, on your right, is now the headquarters of the local branch of the Royal British Legion, the plentiful stone dressings and decorative details of which make it the grandest house in Blandford. Exquisite Lime Tree House (12) opposite is a classic example of the finest in Georgian architecture.

Go through to the Tabernacle with its oak tree, below which is mounted a stone (13) commemorating the tercentenary of the granting of the Royal Charter in 1605, and the Library which received a Civic Trust award for its intelligent design. Leslie House (14) next to it, is the home of the curate of the Parish Church of St Peter and St Paul.

Further on, in the Close, is the Old House (15) built by a Dr Sagittary sometime between 1650 and 1670. The character of the buildings of his native Germany is expressed by the rusticated brickwork, heavy roof and tall shafted chimney stacks. Dorset Street and Orchard Street, to your left, the site of the original garden of the Old House, contain good examples of 19th century terraced archiecture, now in the official Conservation Area.

An alleyway — with its sign saying 'Cycling Prohibited' — a few yards beyond the Old House leads down to East Street. Some of the smaller houses at the eastern end of East Street were built after an earlier fire, but their tiled roofs enabled them to escape the later one. Eastway House (16) is one exception, with its elegant front set back, highlighting the imposing door, decorative urns and front railings.

Returning along East Street, note the growth in scale of the houses, among them Lyston House (17) to your right, and Stour House (18) with its long garden going down to the river, on your left. The road then curves gently to reveal the full beauty and splendour of the Parish Church, and the lovely Georgian terraces of the Market Place. Go up Sheep Market Hill to the Rectory (19). The mythical story of a headless sheep, supposed to run up and down at midnight, must date from 1822, when the market was moved out of the town. The garden wall to the north of the Churchyard includes the entrance (20) to the original Church Almshouses, now blocked up by the present owners of Old Bank House at the west end of the wall and awaiting restoration.

There is an obelisk in the Churchyard commemorating the Bastard family, builders of what proved to be one of the late Sir John Betjeman's favourite churches. To appreciate the church to the full, go in

The Church of St Peter and St Paul, Blandford Forum.

by the west door where a guide book will be found, and, on leaving, you will see the monument to the last fire, a Town Pump, erected by the Bastard brothers, and designed to provide water in perpetuity to itinerant travellers.

Opposite the church tower is a yard known as Bere's Yard, down which, on the right hand side, is the Museum (21), opened in April 1985 to present a pictorial history of the town from earliest times to the day before yesterday.

Except for Lloyd's Bank, buildings on the south side of the Market Place present a rich variety of the period immediately after the last fire. The three finest examples are the Bastards' own home of bold symmetrical design (22), the Red Lion Inn having capitals on its pillars (23) and the old Greyhound Inn (24), with plaster decoration containing bunches of grapes.

On the north side of the Market Place the stone facade of the Corn Exchange declares its civic importance (25). The triple arches with iron gates curving in reverse, and splendid lanterns, lead through the Shambles to the main meeting hall. If you stand outside the old Greyhound building you can see how closely the pediments, vases and arches of the Corn Exchange are echoed by those of the Church. Return to the Marsh Car Park via Greyhound Yard and Safeways.

Bournemouth

Dorset's premier resort is so large that there is no short all-embracing town trail. There are, however, several interesting walks for those who wish to explore the surrounds.

Central Gardens provide a lovely quiet walk along the Bourne Stream, all the more remarkable because it is in the town centre. There are plenty of seats and resting points; this is a walk to be taken slowly and enjoyed.

To go further afield, follow Westover Road through the Lower Pleasure Gardens, past the Pavilion Theatre and the Bournemouth International Conference Centre, and up the cliff path to West Cliff. Beautiful views open up across to Purbeck, and the Old Harry rocks. Continuing in this direction you can explore Durley, Middle and Alum Chines before turning back to the town centre. The chines are deep valleys full of lush vegetation that cut inland from the sea.

If you have more energy, continue beyond the chines over the shore line. Just past Canford Cliffs a short walk over the sands will take you from Bournemouth to Poole. Still heading in a westerly direction you will arrive at Sandbanks and the floating chain bridge which crosses to Purbeck. A nearby 'bus stop will enable you to find transport back to the town centre (open-topped 'buses in summer), if you can't face the return on foot!

Bridport

The trail starts at St Swithin's Church in North Allington, with its altar unconventionally set at the western end. A Georgian building, it has a grand portico in Athenian style and an elaborate cupola. The interior is large and light, almost of modern appearance, and most unlike everyone's idea of a 'traditional' church.

Turn left along West Street and cross the River Brit to West Mill, which stands on the foundations of a 15th century flour mill. The building now houses an architectural practice, the mill machinery, thankfully, being retained.

Granville House is Bridport's Head Post Office, and has housed doctors and other leading citizens for more than two centuries. An imposing facade with a surprisingly ample space behind, it has bequeathed its beautiful stair rail to Bridport Museum.

The Cancer Research Shop in East Street, which was originally the

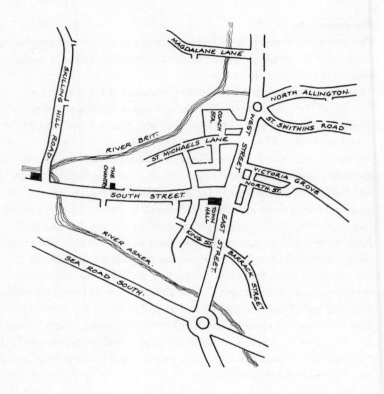

George Inn, is reputed to have been the hostelry at which King Charles stopped briefly while making his escape. It became a pharmacy in 1804, and remained so until the 1960s. The shop front has remained virtually unchanged: bow windows enhance what must be the prettiest facade in Bridport.

Further along on your left, just before the Library, you will find the Unitarian Chapel, set well back from the road. It dates from 1794. On the other side of the street is the United Reformed and Methodist Church.

The Library, imposing stone with lovely arched windows, is in the old Literary and Scientific Institute building.

Continue walking east, taking note of the many fine buildings on both sides of the street. As you approach the east end of town, Bridge House (now an hotel) marks that approach. Built by the

Reverend John Rooker in 1769 as an academy for training independent ministers, it overlooks the bridge which threatens offenders with
transportation for life.

St John's Priory, on the south side of East Street, complements
Bridge House as an entrance to the town. It stands on the site of the
House and Hospital of St John Baptist, a double Order of "Brothers
and Sisters serving God", documented as early as 1240. There is a
Newsagent on the corner. Walk across the bridge and turn right into
Back Rivers Lane. From here you can see the stone built rear exten-
sion, with a small oriel window. This was inserted when the building
passed into private hands.

In 1769 a New Establishment (the Marquis of Granby) was built as
"the best Inn on the Great Western Road", possibly on the medieval
foundations. This later became the "Granby Works", making shoe
uppers, and is now the Masonic Hall. The rather grim facade is next
to the Newsagent, above.

Walk west now, back up the way you have come. Pass the lovely
red brick building with stone quoins and window surrounds, which is
now the premises of a firm of solicitors. This can best be seen from
the other side of the road, especially the decorative parapets and
central pediment.

The Bull Hotel (then the Bull Inn) has a place in the history of the
town. In 1685 a detachment of cavalry and infantry of the Duke of
Monmouth's forces attacked the King's militia in Bridport. Loyalists
fired from the windows of the Bull Inn. The return fire killed Mr
Coker, to whom there is a memorial in St Katherine's Chapel in St
Mary's Church.

Further up, the Greyhound Hotel site has held a tavern since the
14th century. In 1400 it became the property of the community of
Bridport, and remained in the Borough's possession until 1800. It
probably became the Greyhound Inn in Tudor times, when the silver
greyhound was the badge of royal messengers. The archway through
to the yards would have been much used in its days as a coaching inn.

The Town Hall is now ahead of you. No picture of Bridport is
typical unless it includes the wide main street, the Town Hall and
Colmers Hill in the distance. Standing on the site of the Carmelite
chapel of St Andrew, the Town Hall is at the centre of the Medieval
township. Built in 1786 as the Market House, it held 37 butchers'

stalls on the ground floor. This Georgian building is part of the "Pride of Place" of Bridport, and contains several paintings depicting scenes from the history of Bridport. Interested parties should enquire at the Town Council Offices for permission to view.

Turn left into South Street to find the Museum, sometimes known as the Castle. This Tudor building stands on the site of the northern gates of Saxon Bridport. Gutted by fire in 1876, the external walls remained intact and the building was restored. Since 1932 it has housed the Museum and Art Gallery, thanks to Captain Codd of Beaminster. The Museum includes the Rope and Net Collection, representing the trade for which Bridport is world-famous.

Continuing down South Street, the parish church of St Mary stands on the left, at the site of the ancient Saxon crossroads. This 13th century parish church is considered to be one of Dorset's finest, with unusual triple chancel, embattled tower, pinnacles and turrets, and lovely lancet windows. The oldest part of the present building probably dates from the early 14th century and the list of Rectors is continuous since 1317. St Mary's holds the tomb of a 13th century knight in full armour, and the Cross behind the High Altar is decorated with studs, said to represent the pebbles of Chesil Beach. Restoration in 1860 completely changed the interior and partially the external appearance. There is an attractive oriel window over the south porch.

Since the 17th century Bridport has been the home of a community of Quakers, and just a little way further along on your left is the Friends Meeting House. In 1697 the Quaker, Daniel Taylor, gave a barn to the Society of Friends for a permanent Meeting House and some tenements behind as Alms Houses for the poor of the town. Walk through the pleasant courtyard to the peaceful garden and burial ground overlooking the water meadows.

Still heading south, the Chantry is possibly the oldest building in Bridport. Close to the original harbour it may have been a fortified building to protect the southernmost part of the town, although it could also have served as a lighthouse with a cresset, lighting boats up the River Brit. It became a house for priests, who were probably attached to one of the altars in St Mary's to say masses for the repose of the souls of the dead.

There is evidence of an altar on the first floor above the porch, and

Palmer's Brewery, Bridport.

the priests may have carried out their duties without recourse to the parish church. After the Reformation it became a dwelling, continuing as such until 1972. It has been restored recently with the help of English Heritage.

Very few independent private breweries survive today but Palmer's Old Brewery, with its thatched roof, makes it worth walking the extra 300 yards south. Turn along Skilling Hill Road to the back of the brewery to see the water wheel. Opposite, there is a footpath which leads you back along the western river bank past the Football Club and playing fields, across the river by two small bridges, and back to the main car park by the 'bus station.

Christchurch

The Heritage Trail is a guide to Christchurch's rich, interesting history. In a short leisurely stroll you will see all the fascinating and ancient buildings in the centre of Christchurch, as well as scenic views of the rivers, Quay and Mill Stream.

The route is flat and therefore suitable for wheelchairs. However it is advisable to follow the Convent Walk route rather than the alternative route through Priory Gardens.

Start at the Old Town Hall (1), in High Street. This stands at the widest part of the High Street where, from about 1150 to the mid 19th century, a market was held each week. (This now takes place on Mondays to the rear of the High Street.) The Old Town Hall was originally built elsewhere in the High Street, and moved to its present site in the mid 19th century. In 1983, when Saxon Square was built, the archways were re-opened as they had been originally to allow access to the precinct.

The building of the Priory Church (2) commenced in 1094. It is the largest parish church in England and is larger than many cathedrals. The legendary 'Miraculous Beam' may be seen in the roof of the South Quire Aisle. The fish weathervane represents the famous Christchurch Salmon and two of the Priory bells are the oldest in the country to be used regularly.

The Red House Museum and Gardens (3) contains a well presented record of domestic life, industrial activity, geological and natural history, and is well worth a visit. Interesting exhibitions are frequently held in the Art Gallery. The Red House was, at one time, the local workhouse.

It was to Town Quay (4) that Christchurch's coal and timber used to be brought by sailing barge. Today it offers a pleasant riverside walk with picturesque views. In the season there are many entertainments including band concerts, ferry trips and boat hire. Close to the Quay is Christchurch Tricycle Museum which houses many exhibits, mainly from the Victorian era.

Place Mill (5), mentioned in the Domesday Book, ground corn for the town for many centuries. It was much used in the 18th century by smugglers. The working life of the mill continued until early this century when structural defects forced its closure. The mill and

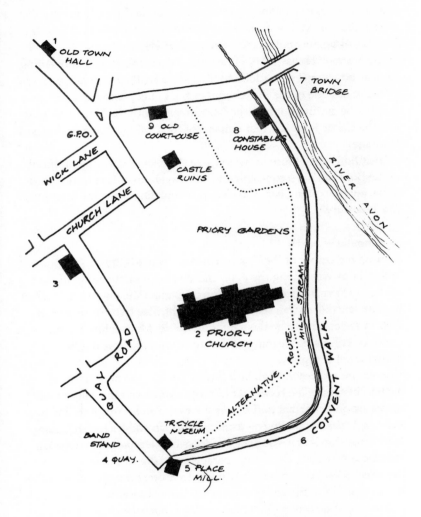

machinery have been carefully restored and open to the public during the summer.

Convent Walk (6) follows the Mill Stream from Town Bridge to Town Quay. It was opened to the public in 1911 to commemorate the Coronation of King George V.

Dating back to the 15th or 16th century, Town Bridge (7) is one of three interesting bridges in Christchurch. The others are nearby:

Waterloo Bridge spanning another branch of the River Avon and the medieval Place Mill Bridge. You will often see many fish in this clear river, and hopeful anglers trying to catch them.

The Norman House (8) is a fine relic of domestic architecture dating from 1160 when it was added to the Castle for the resident Constable. It has one of the first chimneys built in England and a privy or 'garderobe' jutting out into the Mill Stream. Both the Norman House and the Castle Keep (all that remains of the Castle) belong to English Heritage.

The Old Court House (9) was where the Mayor and Chief Officials of the Borough (two constables, bailiff, hayward and ale taster) used to be sworn in each year. This delightful building bears the inscription "12th century".

Dorchester – north

Start on the corner of the Top o' Town cross roads, by the telephone boxes. Look west along the A35, and you are looking along the line of the old Roman road from London to Exeter. The impressive bulk of the Dorset Military Museum is on the right. The twin-towered Keep, built in 1879, used to be the gatehouse to the Dorsetshire Regiment barracks. Following cleaning of the stonework in 1990, it is beautifully floodlit at night.

Looking east, down High East Street, you can see almost to the bottom of town. The tower of St Peter's church and the spire of All Saints are an important part of this view of Dorchester. Note the varying styles of buildings – mainly Georgian and Victorian – many with three storeys plus dormer windows in their mansard roofs. Railings, bow windows, decorative parapets and door canopies add to the street scene, which is mainly given to professional practices rather than shops. Of particular note is the Old Tea House, dated 1623, just inside High East Street on the left, and the lovely brick and stone front of Savernake House, with its magnolia tree.

Walk about 50 yards south of the telephone boxes. Dorchester was defended in Roman times by banks and ditches, topped by walls, and on the left you can see the only surviving section of these Roman walls. A plaque records the gift to Dorchester by Lucia Catharine Stone in 1886, and a nearby descriptive panel shows how the walls encircled the town.

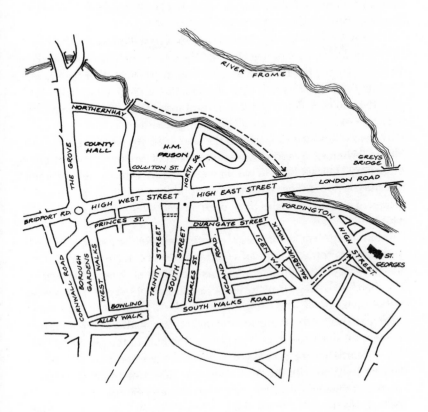

In the early 18th century, in a far-sighted move, walls and banks were levelled and their positions planted with trees. This formed the avenues, or Walks as they are known, which give Dorchester a character unlike any other town.

We are going to walk round the northern outskirts of Dorchester, along the line of the walls, and then cut back through the centre to your starting point.

Cross High East Street and head for Thomas Hardy. This bronze statue was sculpted by Eric Kennington in 1931. It is a pilgrimage for all lovers of Hardy's books who visit the town, and particularly in summer is never short of a tourist or two having their photographs taken. Flowered wreaths commemorating Hardy's contribution to literature often decorate the plinth.

Colliton Walk, originally New Walk, runs past Colliton Park which is now occupied by County Hall and the Library. Ahead you can see how quickly the town becomes open countryside, another feature of Dorchester which makes it such an attractive place in which to live.

At the end of Colliton Walk turn right into Northernhay, the old North Walk. A gate in the wall on the right leads into Colliton Park behind County Hall, and to the site of the Roman Town House. When excavations were undertaken before the construction of County Hall, six Roman buildings were discovered including some fine mosaic floors. The remains of one building can be seen, and one mosaic. The other mosaics have been moved safely to the County Museum.

Return to the Walks through the gate, and take the path down to the River Frome. Hangman's Cottage (17th century) featured in Hardy's story 'The Withered Arm' as the home of the executioner. The thatched cottage is picturesque, and is one of very few remaining in the town.

The path now runs alongside the mill stream, with a view of Dorchester as it skirts the river. You can see the bulk of the prison buildings in North Square, where you will walk in due course. Eventually, the path joins up with the A35, emerging alongside the White Hart.

In the distance on your left you can see Grey's Bridge, the eastern approach to the town. It was built in 1748 when a new road was built across the water-meadows. All London traffic prior to that date went through Fordingon's narrow streets. Right, the view uphill to your starting point. It is a gentle walk, with much to see and admire on the way.

On the left is the narrow entrance to Fordington High Street and, through Salisbury Street, to Salisbury Fields. (See Dorchester South Trail.) Further up, on the corner of Church Street, is All Saints Church with its beautiful spire. The spire can be seen from every approach to the town, and features on the Dorchester town signs erected by the roadsides.

All Saints was built in 1845, on the site of a 17th century building which had been demolished in 1843. The rebuilding cost £3,000!

Now de-consecrated, the church is used to store the archaeological collections of the County Museum.

Icen Way, on the left, was once Gaol Lane. It leads through to South Walks, at which junction the gallows stood. One of Dorchester's prisons was sited on the corner, and No 12 High East Street and Nos 1 and 2 Icen Way are believed to incorporate stone from that prison.

On the opposite side of the road, the Kings Arms Hotel has a prominent and important position. It was in this hotel that the Mayors's dinner at the beginning of Hardy's novel *The Mayor of Casterbridge* was held. The broad columned porch with bow window above enhance a facade that has changed little over the years.

Beyond the Kings Arms stands the Corn Exchange with Town Hall over. Built in 1847/8, the corner clock tower was added to the building in 1864. It was partly financed by Alderman Galpin. Because the tower seemed to have no substantial support, townspeople named it 'Galpin's folly'. Despite their scepticism, it is still there.

Turn right into North Square, and Friary Hill will take you down for a look at the River Frome where you walked earlier. The prison is the second one to be built on this site. The old County Gaol was demolished in the late 18th century, and the prison rebuilt and enlarged. There is a Portland stone gateway to the north and this, and part of the walls, are all that survive of the original buildings.

Colliton Street, branching off the Square, used to be Pease Lane in the 19th century. One of the cottages in the street has a plaque commemorating John White. It is thanks to him that the settlement of New Dorchester, Massachusetts was formed. He raised money and sought a charter for the would-be colonists from Charles I, forming the emigrants into a church society to face the dangers ahead. The church in Dorchester, Boston, built with their thanks, is still known as the 'Daughter of John White'.

Return from North Square to High East Street. Opposite is South Street, the main shopping street, with the town pump in the centre. We are going to continue walking west, uphill, where High East Street now becomes High West Street.

St Peter's church, with its tower, is the only surviving medieval church in Dorchester. It is mostly 15th century, and restoration in 1991 has given new life to some of the gargoyles and decorative pinnacles. There is a statue of the Dorset poet, William Barnes, in the churchyard.

The Dorset County Museum, built in the 1880s, is a lovely Victorian building. It stands next to Holy Trinity Church. This church had simple lines and a low tower prior to 1824, when a much more ornate Gothic building took its place. In 1875 the present building, designed by Benjamin Ferrey, was built.

Opposite, Judge Jeffreys' Lodging House is a half-timbered house which dates from the early 17th century. The Judge is 'famous' for his Bloody Assizes, when retribution was exacted on the followers of the Monmouth Rebellion. The assize sermon was read in St Peter's Church opposite, and was followed by the impaling of a human head on the railings outside. The sermon is still read at the start of the assizes in the town, but the second part has been dispensed with!

On the same side as Judge Jeffreys, crossing over Trinity Street, is the Old Ship Inn, the oldest pub in Dorchester. Dating from the early 17th century, it has been much altered and reconstructed. Beyond it, the Royal Oak pub which has served the town for over 300 years. The arch leading through to the yards is evidence that it played its part as a coaching inn.

Opposite are the offices of West Dorset District Council. The old Shire Hall was built in 1796/7, and the Old Crown Court within has its original fittings. It was opened to the public in 1956 as a memorial to the Tolpuddle Martyrs, who stood trial there in 1834.

On the east end of the building you can see the mileages from that point to Hyde Park Corner, Blandford and Bridport. It is interesting to note that although the road network must have changed considerably since those times the mileages, particularly to London, are still fairly accurate.

Just a short distance further and you arrive back at your starting point. To explore the southern half of the town in the same way, by the Walks and then the centre, follow the Dorchester South Trail. Hopefully you will find it every bit as interesting.

Dorchester – South

At the same starting point as the other Dorchester trail, by the telephone boxes at Top o' Town, begin your walk by heading south past the section of Roman wall on your left. This was given to the town by Lucia Catharine Stone in 1886, and a descriptive panel nearby shows how the walls enclosed the Roman town of Durnovaria.

Cross Princes Street. Still walking south, you have a choice of keeping in the shade of the trees in West Walks, or cutting through the Borough Gardens. The gardens were laid out in 1895, and the bandstand erected three years later. Note the decorative clock, made in the foundry of Lott & Walne at the end of Fordington High Street.

The decorative clock, the Borough Gardens, Dorchester.

At the southern end of the gardens or the Walks, turn left into Bowling Alley Walk and follow it along to its junction with Trinity Street. You are still following the line of the Roman walls. Cross Trinity and South Streets for a look a the War Memorial, and also to note the six-sided Victorian letterbox nearby. It is one of the oldest in the county.

Take a good look, too, at the premises of James Foot Ltd with its traditionally grained exterior. The shop is as traditional inside – no plastic-coated modernity – and the service is as good as one would expect.

We will walk a short distance up South Street, as far as the end of Hardye Arcade. This was named after yet another Hardye in Dorchester, who founded a grammar school which once stood on this site. Glance up at the buildings opposite the end of the arcade and read two plaques. You will see that Thomas Hardy worked as a pupil to John Hicks, Architect, from 1856 – 1862; William Barnes, Dorset's much-loved poet, lived next door from 1847 – 1862.

Just a little way further up on your right is Nappers Mite, with its distinctive clock. This was an almshouse built by Sir Robert Napper in 1615. The facade was rebuilt in 1842, and in recent years the courtyard has been opened through to a small development of shops at the rear. Walk through to Charles Street, and turn right to rejoin South Walks over the pedestrianised area by the car park. (Please note that, out of shopping hours, the way through Nappers Mite is locked. In this case retrace your steps to Hardye Arcade and use that to cut through to Charles Street as before.)

Turn left to continue along South Walks, and glance across the town to your left. You can see Dorchester's three distinctive landmarks: the tower of St Peter's Church, the clock tower on the Corn Exchange, and the spire of All Saints Church.

At the end of Icen Way, once called Gaol Lane, and on the site of the gallows, there is a scupture by Dame Elisabeth Frink. Two martyrs face a personification of Death, in memory of those who suffered in Dorset in the religious troubles of the 16th and 17th centuries.

You now have the option of a shorter walk, turning left into Salisbury Fields, or of continuing straight on for a look at St George's Church, Fordington, and a walk down Fordington High Street.

The shorter version takes you through the Fields with the Armada

Beacon, and out at the far end into Salisbury Street, noting the attractive terrace of houses on your right as you pass. They are built of a popular local brick known as Broadmayne, named after the village where they were made. The brickworks is no longer there, and 'Broadmaynes' from buildings being demolished are much sought after for renovation work within the area. We will be turning left into Durngate Street, and this is where the longer walk rejoins the route.

The 'optional extra' goes straight ahead at the Martyrs, heading for St George's which you can see ahead of you. On your right is a lovely terrace of cottages with their decorative date plaques of 1886.

St George's Church started life of very modest size, but was greatly enlarged between 1907 – 1912. This was its seventh restoration, and the interior is worthy of detailed exploration. During the building works footings were found of what may have been a Saxon church and, from even earlier times, a Roman tombstone. The inscribed marble slab can be seen on the wall of the inner tower.

Over the south door, studded 1717, is an unusual panel depicting St George. The style is reminiscent of the Bayeux Tapestry – a strangely appropriate connection, since Dorchester is twinned with Bayeux in France.

On leaving the church, and having enjoyed the views around Fordington Green, turn right to walk the length of Fordington High Street. There are some lovely houses: note Dunloe House on your left, with its door canopy and double bay windows. Further on down the High Street is a raised pavement and railings, recently restored.

Fordington used to be the 'poor' area of the town, heavily populated and without any sanitary provisions. Disease was rife, including two outbreaks of cholera in 1849 and 1854. The latter outbreak spread from the barracks at the Top o'Town, in dirty clothes that were brought down to Fordington to be washed.

The Vicar at that time, Henry Moule, was instrumental in bringing about many changes for the better in his parish. His fight against cholera – and against other 'evils' in the town such as beer and racing! – was the subject of Dorchester's first Community Play, "Entertaining Strangers". This play, an enormous success in the county, later transferred to the National Theatre with Dame Judy Dench. Many a coachload went from Dorchester to see the town's history so movingly depicted.

At the bottom of the High Street, turn left by the fish and chip shop into Salisbury Street, and right into Durngate Street, joining the shorter walk here.

Where Durngate Street crosses Icen Way you will see the Dinosaur Museum on the corner. The only museum in the country devoted to dinosaurs, it makes a fascinating visit, especially for children.

At the junction of Durngate Street and Acland Road is one of Dorchester's most attractive houses, Wollaston House. Until 1858 Wollaston House was set in grounds of 8 acres, stretching back to the Walks. It was built in 1786 and names after Charlton Byam Wollaston, one of the Grand Jury who tried the Tolpuddle Martyrs.

Continue straight on, along Durngate Street, to the town's main shopping area of South Street. If you have time, go 100 yards to your left to see the lovely building that houses Barclays Bank. To the right, at the top of South Street known as Cornhill, is the town pump. Note also the 18th century red brick fronts to the buildings, many of which were altered beyond recognition further down the street.

The Antelope Hotel dates from 1815, and it was here that Judge Jeffreys held the Bloody Assizes which brought many of the followers of the Monmouth Rebellion to 'justice'. The Antelope and its yard were the subject of much rebuilding in 1990, and the arcade of shops stretching through to Trinity Street received the West Dorset District Council Civic Design award. The developers were required to reinstate the original Antelope sign at the entrance, but many people regret the passing of the old grape vine that used to shade the (replaced) glass canopy of the yard.

At Trinity Street, turn right to regain High West Street. If you have not already followed the Dorchester North trail, you will find in it details of notable buildings between here and Top o' Town where you began the walk.

We will make one final small detour for those with the stamina! Just past the District Council offices on the right, turn right into Glyde Path Road. On your right you will come to Colliton Street, and from the corner of Colliton Street stretches a most attractive terrace of cottages, all different.

On your left, the bulk of Colliton House. It was one of Dorchester's most important houses, and stood in extensive parkland. Colliton Park was developed, and the Library and County Hall now cover a substantial part of the grounds.

Tun left to walk past the Library, left into Colliton Walk, and you will see ahead of you the telephone boxes where you began your walk.

Lyme Regis – The Monmouth Trail

On 24 May 1685 James, Duke of Monmouth, set sail for England to contest the throne of his uncle James II. The rebellion lasted two short months, with hundreds of vanquished supporters coming before the infamous Judge Jeffreys at his Bloody Assizes held in Dorchester.

The fleet bringing the Duke of Monmouth to England was first sited from the Bowling Green at Lyme Regis, just above where Langmoor Gardens now stand. Monmouth landed on the beach immediately west of the Cobb, and rode inland at the head of about 2000 men.

Despite an interval of 300 years the route which Monmouth and his supporters took into Lyme Regis can still be followed by visitors today.

Start at Monmouth Beach near the Cobb, where the Duke landed and where 12 of his supporters were later hanged. From the car park walk up Cobb Road and turn right onto the public footpath leading to the mini golf course. Turning left into Stile Lane, follow the lane uphill through the trees to the site of the old Bowling Green on your left near the top. From here Monmouth's ships were first sited on 11 June 1685.

Turn right along Pound Street and walk downhill to the bottom of Broad Street. Here lay the old Market Place, marked by a wall plaque on the left-hand side of the street, where the declaration denouncing James II was read to the assembled townspeople on the day after Monmouth's landing.

Across Broad Street is Cobb Gate. The old canon sited here would originally have stood at Gun Cliff with the main town batteries which persuaded Monmouth to land further west than he might have done. The Cliff can be seen just to the east of Cobb Gate car park. Walk up

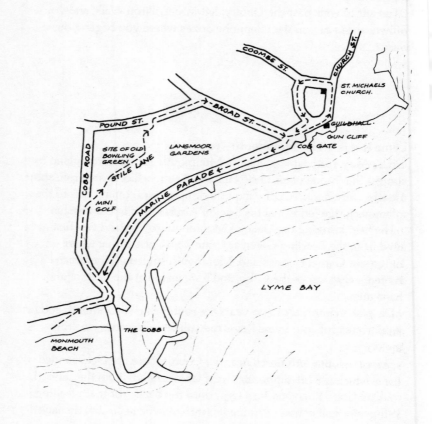

Bridge Street to the Guildhall (containing the Tourist Information Centre) and Gun Cliff, both marked by commemorative wall plaques, and turn left into Church Street. At the old Buttermarket (indicated by a wall plaque) half way up the street are a row of 17th century houses which would have been standing in Monmouth's time.

Carry on up Church Street, past the Church itself, and turn left into Monmouth Street. On the corner is the 350 year old Old Monmouth Hotel, once a coaching inn and reputed to have been the billet for Monmouth's cavalry under Lord Grey.

From here you may either take the left-hand path into George's Square, the old inn yard, and through the passage into Coombe Street, or carry on along Monmouth Street and left into Coombe Street. At No 37 is the site of the George Inn, commemorated by a wall plaque, which provided lodgings for Monmouth during his stay in Lyme.

Returning along Coombe Street to Bridge Street, you may like to visit the Philpot Museum opposite, which contains many fascinating relics of the town's history and prehistory.

If you would like to see something of Monmouth in the other side of the county, start at Wimborne Minster. In the wall of the Minster lies the body of Anthony Etrrick, the magistrate whose order sent the Duke to London to his death.

Drive north towards Cranborne until you reach the Horton Inn, and turn right. After nearly 3 miles you reach a bridge at the beginning of the hamlet of Horton Heath. On your left lies the "Island", and area of cultivated ground in Monmouth's time in the midst of a tract of barren heathland. Here Monmouth was found cowering in a ditch beneath a tall ash tree. Although the ash tree has long since died of old age, the spot has ever afterwards been known as Monmouth's Ash. There is no public access to Monmouth's Ash, but the footpath up Slough Lane, beside the bridge, leads to Peat's Hill, an attractive spot for viewing the area. (Please do not take your car up Slough Lane, which is a private road.)

Poole

Many of Poole's old buildings have been demolished, and the only really compact group of interesting buildings is in the Conservation Area adjacent to the Quay.

St James in Thames Street, Poole's parish church, has a beautiful Georgian interior. It was rebuilt in 1880, and the unique Newfoundland wood pillars are a reminder of Poole's trading links. St James is usually open Saturday mornings, or by appointment through the Tourism Centre (0202-672694). The King Charles pub is late 16th century, but has undergone much restoration.

· Take time to look at West End House and the Mansion House. The latter is one of the largest houses built by the merchants of Poole in 1800, and is now a hotel.

Off Thames Street, Market Street leads to the Guildhall (1761) with its lovely curved external staircases. Mid-eighteenth century, the Guildhall used to house a meat market on the open lower floor. It is now used for exhibitions of local interest. Byngley House in Market Street is 400 years old, and is said to be haunted.

Back on the Quay the Customs House also has an attractive entrance, with steps leading up to the columned porch at first floor level. The nearby Town Cellars, now a museum, and Harbour Office form an interesting group.

Shaftesbury

An ancient Saxon hilltop town, claims the sign as you enter Shaftesbury, with considerable justification. Known in Celtic times as Caer Palladwr, then Sceapterbyrig, in 880 after the defeat of the Vikings, King Alfred built here on this greenstone escarpment a burgh, and about 888 an Abbey. Scafton became Shaston and now Shaftesbury. 700 feet above sea level, with commanding views over the surrounding countryside, it was for a time Alfred's capital, till he pushed eastwards to Winchester and London.

The town has many interesting features, including the now famous Gold Hill, the steeply cobbled street, located behind the Town Hall. It is a popular location for artists, film makers and photographers. The top of the hill makes a good starting point for a walk of discovery. With the Sun and Moon cottage on the left and the local museum housed in what was once a doss house, the massively buttressd medieval enclosure wall of the Abbey on the right, with a view over the valley stretching out beyond the hilltops, a step or two back in time is not as fanciful as it might seem.

Taking those steps down the hill, notice the cottages on the east side, each one supporting its neighbour. Some may have been shops, and Shaftesbury is known to have had three mints at one point with one of them on the hill. Stalls would also have been set up on the west side between the buttresses of the wall. Having reached the bottom, turn right and walk along St James's.

Above you on the right is the steep slope of the escarpment and to your left as you walk the Two Brewers Inn. Further along on the right is the Pumpyard or Andrew's Yard, a courtyard of old thatched cot-

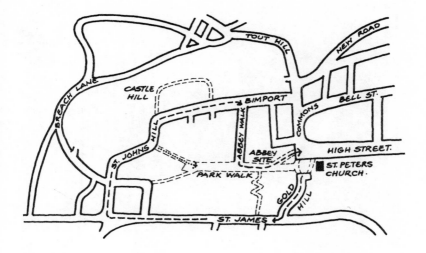

tages with a pump in the centre.

Proceeding along to Tanyard Lane the visitor has the option of turning right and following Stoney Path up the hill to Park Walk, or continuing along St James's to the school and church on the corner. Turn right and follow the road up St John's Hill, on the last bend is the churchyard with its ancient yew tree, and just beyond a further option.

Some visitors may wish to proceed through the gate onto the north facing walk of the town called Castle Hill, or just follow the road. There is the site of an ancient earthwork on the western edge of Castle Hill and the settlement at the foot of the hill is Enmore Green.

Notice the Fountain Inn, which is the site of the fresh water well that supplied the town with its drinking water. Water is the reason for an ancient ceremony in Shaftesbury called the Bysant, a contract between the citizens of the town and the Lord of Gillingham, who . owned the settlement of Enmore Green where the wells were located. Water was taken up the hill to Shaftesbury probably on donkey panniers and sold in much the same way as fresh milk was carried around London's streets.

A panoramic dial here and another on Park Walk indicate some of the vantage points to be seen from these view areas.

Gold Hill, Shaftesbury.

Abbey) and walking east, on the left stands Ox House, featured in the novel *Jude the Obscure* by Thomas Hardy. Just after this point turn right by the old school (now flats) and proceed into Abbey Walk. The old Schoolhouse is on the left with the Westminster Memorial Hospital on the right. This brings you to the War Memorial, after the style of many Celtic crosses, and Park Walk.

Here again are spectacular views over the valley to Melbury Beacon and the uplands of Cranborne Chase, a medieval hunting ground.

The Abbey ruins are behind the wall to your left and it is thought that the cloister extends under part of Park Walk. The Abbey was very famous in medieval times as a centre of pilgrimage to see the bones of St Edward, King and Martyr who was killed at Corfe, and his remains translated here from Wareham, a sister house to Shaftesbury.

Canute died here and was buried at Winchester. Another Royal visitor was Katherine of Aragon, on her way to marry Prince Arthur, brother of Henry VIII who was responsible for the Dissolution of the Monasteries and our Abbey.

The Abbey buildings were totally demolished for building stone, and the town went into a decline. Shaftesbury also lost its button industry, after manufactured buttons were displayed at the Great Exhibition in 1851.

Returning to the centre of town, note the Grosvenor Hotel in the Commons which houses the Chevy Chase sideboard. Round off the walk with a visit to St Peter's Church and admire the lierne vault dating from the 15th century in the west porch.

Shaftesbury is not a place of fossiled history, but a living town with many clubs and activities. It is twinned with Brionne in Normandy and Lindlar in West Germany.

Sherborne

Both a long and short walk begin in the same way. Starting in Cheap Street, look for the Conduit at the south end. This hexagonal structure was built in the early 16th century by Abbot Mere of Sherborne, and served as the monks' wash-house or lavatorium. Originally placed among the monastic buildings behind the Abbey, after the Dissolution of the Monasteries it was moved to its present position, where it provided water for the townspeople.

During the Civil War and while nearby Dorchester sided with the Parliamentarians, Sherborne's rulers saw to it that the town remained fiercely royalist, and on the restoration of Charles II the Conduit gave up its usual function and 'ran with clarret besides many hogsheads of March Bear'. Since then the Conduit has served many purposes, during the nineteenth century becoming in turn a reading room, a sub post office, a police station and a bank. In 1933 the Governors of Sherborne School gave the building to the town.

Behind the Conduit notice the half-timbered building of Bow House, formerly the Sun Inn and now housing the staff room of Sherborne School.

From the Conduit walk towards Bow House, and keep left into Church Lane, a pedestrian way. On the left is the town's Museum, reached by passing under the 15th century Cemetery gate or Bow Arch. The Museum contains a good collection of photographs and

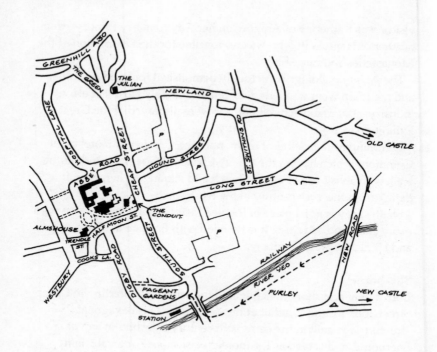

exhibits illustrating local history.

A little further down and on the right can be seen the original entrance to Sherborne School. The school, which is known locally as the 'King's School', was re-founded in 1550 by Edward VI when, after the Reformation, the Government was looking for new schools to teach Protestantism and loyalty to the Crown, replacing the educational system which had previously been provided by the monks. This 'Free Grammar School of King Edward VI' was run by a board of governors in much the same way as the town's almshouse, providing free education for local children and making up the financial shortfall by taking boarders from outside the town, usually wealthy landowners' and tradesmens' sons, who gradually became the majority.

In 1871 the passing of the Endowed Schools Bill allowed its establishment as an independent public school, revoking the requirement that governors should be townsmen and abolishing free places. Over the wall can be seen the Old Schoolroom, completed in 1608.

From Church Lane walk into the Churchyard, noting the handsome

The Conduit, Sherborne.

wrought iron gates (1723). The Churchyard was the town's cemetery until 1856, when the present grounds in Lenthay were opened. On the right is the magnificent Abbey Church of Saint Mary the Virgin. The present building is on the site of an earlier Saxon cathedral.

In AD 705 Saint Aldhelm became the first bishop of Sherborne when he was sent to the town by Ine, King of the West Saxons. The choice of the town probably indicates that there was an earlier Celtic Christian settlement here. The cathedral was a church of secular canons until 998, when the Benedictine rule was introduced by Saint

Wulfsin as part of the reforms of the English Church being carried out by Saint Dunstan of Canterbury, following its decline during the wars with the Danes. Sherborne ceased to be a cathedral city in 1075 when the bishopric was removed to Old Sarum, although the monks remained until the Protestant Reformation.

Go into the Abbey through the South Door. The most important thing to notice is the roof, which contains some of the finest fan vaulting in the country.

On leaving the Abbey follow the path southwards through the Abbey Close to the corner of Trendle and Half Moon Streets, pausing to admire the delightful houses on the west side, mostly 17th century, which form one edge of the Close. On the corner stands the Almshouse of St John the Baptist and Saint John the Evangelist. Though still serving its original function, it is open to the public during the summer and is well worth a visit.

Retrace your steps through the Abbey Close, to the west door of the Abbey. Here is the former site of the Church of All Hallows, demolished after the Dissolution. Although originally only a chapel-of-ease for the Abbey, this 14th century building was about the size of the present Abbey nave and served the townspeople, replacing the earlier church of Saint Aldhelm.

Leaving the Abbey Close through the kissing gate on the right, follow the Abbey Road round the bend to the main gateway of Sherborne School. The arms above the arch with their Welsh dragon are those of the Tudor King Edward VI. Through the arch there is a good view of the north side of the Abbey and the former monastic site, now the school courts.

Continue along Abbey Road and round the corner to regain access to Cheap Street. The town's main street ('Chepe' meaning market), it contains some attractive 16th, 17th and 18th century buildings. In 1643 Cheap Street was turned into a battlefield when a small Parliamentary force under the command of Hugh Popham was set upon by a mob of around three hundred townsmen. With cries of 'Kill the Parliamentary dogs!' and with some of them firing on the soldiers from upstairs windows, the townspeople succeeded in mortally wounding Popham and the troops withdrew to the safety of their main force, commanded by his father and stationed at Yeovil. Three days later Colonel Popham entered Sherborne with these troops and, no doubt spurred on by motives of revenge, organised the systematic plundering of its houses from which the people fled in terror.

(Longer walk addition – the short walk continues at **)

Turning left at the corner of Abbey Road, walk up to the top of Cheap Street to The Julian, an intriguing 16th century hospice building. Now a craft shop, the present house is a replacement of the original 'Julianys Inne' given by Margaret Goffe to the Almshouse in 1438. The interior is charmingly adapted to its present use. Note also the triangular 'splash-back stone' on the exterior corner, designed to prevent public nuisance before the provision of public lavatories.

Retracing your steps briefly down Cheap Street, take the left hand turning into Newland, the result of 13th century property speculation on the part of one of the bishops of Salisbury, and a medieval borough. Walk down on the left hand side to Sherborne House, now Lord Digby's School, formerly the home of the great 19th century Shakespearian actor William Macready and a fine 18th century house. Further down on this side is the Manor House, a much-restored late medieval building which houses the Town and District Council offices. The present name was acquired when a 19th century owner moved here from the Manor House in the nearby village of Trent. A little further down on the right hand side, Newland garden was once the market place.

Interesting houses of different dates line Newland down to the Black Horse Hotel, at the junction with Long Street and Oborne Road. Cross the staggered junction to Castleton Road, signposted 'Sherborne Old Castle'. Take the road over the railway bridge to the gates of the castle ruins, noting the attractive huddle of 17th century houses on the right. Pass through the gates to visit the Old Castle (small charge).

Demolished by order of Parliament during the Commonwealth, the Castle was the work of the 12th century Roger of Caen, Bishop of Sarum, Chancellor to Henry I. Passing into the hands of the monarchy it was eventually regained by Bishop Robert Wyville for the diocese in 1354, in whose hands it stayed until Queen Elizabeth granted it to Sir Walter Raleigh in 1592.

Raleigh seems to have found the experience of living in the Nor-

man castle frustrating. In the end he gave up his attempt to modern-
ise it in favour of building his new Sherborne Lodge, the earliest part
of the New castle which can be seen from the south side of the ruins.

After Raleigh's execution the castle estates were bought by the
Digby family. Being more defensible than the New castle, it was
garrisoned and held for the king during the Civil War, finally falling
to the Parliamentarians on 15 August 1645. Despite the Digby's
royalist sympathies the townspeople seem to have been quite happy
to buy the loot from the Castle next day in the market.

Leaving the Old castle, visit the charming 18th century Church of
St Mary Magdalen on the right, before turning left again into New
Road. After crossing the railway bridge, and if it is not too muddy,
take the pleasant footpath following the south bank of the River Yeo
through the field called Purley. This will take you out through the
gate on to Gas House Hill just above the railway line. If you turn left,
walk up the slope and turn right into New Road, you will soon find a
particularly good view of the town. To get back into the town retrace
your steps to Gas House Hill and cross the railway line, turning left
into Digby Road, and go through the iron gate opposite the railway
station into Pageant Gardens.

** To continue the shorter walk, follow Cheap Street past the Conduit to the corner of Half Moon Street and follow this road across the
front of the Abbey. Just before the Churchyard and on the right is the
Church House, built in 1532 with a row of shops on the ground floor,
and a large open church hall, now sadly subdivided, above. Walk on
past the War Memorial and cross over to walk down Digby Road to
the Pageant Gardens, entered through an iron gate on the left. The
gardens take their name from the great Pageant held in 1905 to
commemorate the twelfth centenary of the town's foundation by
Saint Aldhelm, an occasion recorded on one of the earliest cine films,
of which there is a copy in the County Museum in Dorchester. With
their fine trees and flowers and picturesque bandstand with mature
wisteria, the gardens make a pleasant place to stop for a rest. The land
for the gardens was given by Frederick Wingfield Digby in memory
of his father.

Returning to Digby Road you will see opposite the former Digby
Hotel, now a boarding house belonging to Sherborne School. The

hotel seems to have been the one which appears as 'The Earl of Wessex' in Thomas Hardy's 'The Woodlanders', offering 'the best accommodation in Sherton – having been rebuilt contemporarily with the construction of the railway'. Notice the ostrich emblem of the Digby family on the gables, and massive stable block, now a garage.

Returning up Digby Road towards the Abbey, take the turning into Cooks Lane on the left. The 16th century Digby Tap was once the parish workhouse before becoming the taphouse for the Digby Hotel, providing beer and food for the coachmen and servants of the affluent guests.

At the end of Cooks lane turn right into Westbury. Opposite is the Britannia Inn, part of which was the original Lord Digby's School where poor girls were instructed in reading and sewing. Notice the commemorative tablet above the doorway. Follow Westbury to the Almshouse to regain access to Half Moon Street and Cheap Street, taking a last look at the Abbey before arriving back at the Conduit.

Swanage

The trail starts at the TIC in Shore Road. Turn right out of the garden and walk to the King Alfred Monument. This was erected by John Mowlem, a poor quarryboy who left Swanage to seek his fortune in London and who founded the firm of contractors which still bears his name. The Mowlem replaced the original Institute built by John Mowlem on his retirement to the town.

Walk on along the seafront. The Parade was originally a row of boarding houses built on the site of old stone yards. Swanage grew up around the quarrying of Portland limestone from the cliffs and Purbeck limestone from underground quarries. The stone was transported to the stone yards for dressing before being shipped to many parts of the country. Beyond the Square a set of tramlines can be seen in the road. These were installed to help the transport of stone from the yards to the old pier.

Carry on to the stone quay built to serve the Royal Victoria Hotel, now private flats and several bars. This was one of Swanage's first hotels and its name commemorated the stay of Princess Victoria here in 1833. Further along the sea front the new pier was opened in 1896 with a proper landing-stage for the passenger steamers.

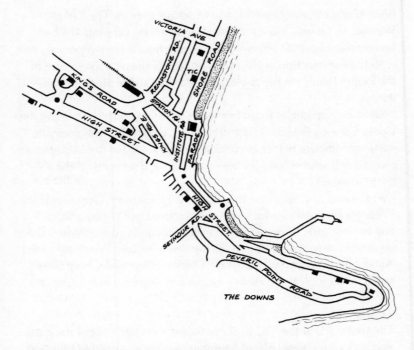

The trail continues along the seaside public footpath by the sailing club, and past the new development at Swanage Haven. Walk on to find the Wellington Clock Tower. This was brought here - without the clock - from near London Bridge in 1867. The original spire became unsafe and was replaced by the present cupola around 1904. Walking on along the seafront you pass first the Lifeboat House and then the old Preventative Station.

Continue on to Peveril Point where stone steps take you up to the Coastguard Lookout. Walk back towards the town along Peveril Point Road through the car park area. At Seymour Road walk down to the High Street. Beyond the Victoria is Victoria Terrace. Number 2 was the home of John Mowlem. He used the rooftop turret room as an astronomical observatory.

Walk along to the White Swan and turn right along Institute Road, named after the original Mowlem Institute. At the end turn left into Station Road then left again at the roundabout and on along Kings Road past the Post Office. Notice the canalised brook which was once a broad marshy inlet of the sea. Follow it along to St Mary's Church. The tower is the oldest part of the church. It was once a fortified defence for the old village.

Cross the brook here and walk up Church Hill, passing the Tithe Barn Museum. West of the church is the old Mill Pond and associated buildings. This is the oldest part of Swanage. A settlement existed here as long ago as 877, supposedly associated with an ancient Royal Swannery. The trail continues up Church Hill to meet the High Street again at the Sir Reginald Palgrave Cross.

Across the street the Black Swan, formerly the Quarrymans' Arms, bears a reminder of the importance of the stone industry in the town's history.

Turn left back down the High Street towards the sea again to find number 91, Purbeck House. This was built by George Burt, the nephew of John Mowlem and his successor in the Company. He became one of Swanage's major benefactors in the late 1800s. Purbeck House is now a convent.

A short distance further on is the Town Hall. The 1670 facade came from the Mercers Hall in London and was brought here by George Burt. Turn left into Town Hall Lane to find the old lock-up. This tiny prison was formerly sited by the church and bears an interesting inscription and the date of erection, 1803.

Carry on down the lane and turn left into Kings Road East. At the end you are back in the town centre again. Cross over Kings Road and go onto the Railway Station platform. The branch line from Wareham was opened in 1885 following strenuous efforts by Mowlem and Burt. It was closed in 1972. Steam enthusiasts have since succeeded in re-opening part of the track with the aim of eventually linking back to the main line.

Having explored the station, turn left into Rempstone Road, part of the new town which expanded rapidly after the arrival of the trains. They brought new building materials and thousands of Victorian holidaymakers to Swanage.

Turn right into Victoria Avenue then right again onto the Recreation Ground to end the trail at the War Memorial, a curious pile of Purbeck stone. From here you can see much of the town that you have explored, as well as lovely views of the chalk cliffs of Ballard Down to the north and the Isle of Wight to the east.

Weymouth

1. Chapelhay to the Nothe

Start at the Old Town Hall, High West Street, behind the fire station. It dates from the 17th century, and was extensively restored in 1896. Behind it is the Coffee Tavern of 1875, built as a temperence 'pub'. Behind you is what remains of one of the main streets of old Weymouth with its terrace of mainly 18th and 19th century houses. Look up Love Lane for another glimpse of the old town. Walk up the steps to the right of the Old Town Hall, leaving the modern block of flats on your right, and on your left in the garden the remains of the heart of Old Weymouth with its modern municipal offices lying below. Beyond lies the inner harbour and Radipole Lake backed by the Ridgeway, beyond which lies Dorchester.

Ahead see the western elevation of Holy Trinity Church (1836) by Philip Wyatt, extended by the local architect G R Crickmay in 1886. The north front faces Melcombe Regis and dominates the approach to the Town Bridge.

Go up the steps to the right and then to the left behind the church and enter Trinity Terrace. These small houses, some dating from the 1830s, look from their bow windows over the town and northwards across Weymouth Bay towards White Nothe and the chalk cliffs.

In the immediate foreground are the backs of the late Georgian houses fronting Trinity Road and the harbour; parts of some of these houses date from much earlier times. In the back plots of some are fragments of walling of still earlier dwellings, 16th century, which overlooked the harbour before the quays were built.

Turn right into Hartlebury Terrace (mid 19th century) then left into Herbert Place and down the steep slope into Hope Square. On the left as you enter the square is Trinity Street. No 3, known as Tudor House, dates from about 1570 - 1600; a typical late town house of a man of means, perhaps a local merchant. It has furniture of the period and is open to the public.

On your right is the imposing front of Brewer's Quay, once Devenish Brewery. This very interesting complex dating variously from 1869 to the grand Dutch gabled facade of 1904 contains the Timewalk, Weymouth's Museum and a museum of brewing. Across the square you can see Pilgrim House, an elegant Georgian house, and to the left a little way down Hope Street, No 6, an earlier but

equally grand town house. Behind them are some of the old mal-
thouses and standing above, the late 18th century barracks now
converted to flats, Wellington Court.

Now cross the square and follow the road round to the right to
Horsford Street. Here you will see facing you Nos 38 and 39, a fine
pair of Regency cottages. Climb up Horsford Street and continue
straight ahead up Belmont Street and into the gardens overlooking
Portland Harbour. Turn left along Jubilee Walk, through the gardens
to Elizabethan Way and thence to the Nothe Fort at the end of the
Nothe peninsula. This coastal defence fort was completed in 1872
under Lord Palmerston's programme of re-arming against possible
French invasion. It was armed with heavy muzzle-loading guns. It is
open to the public.

Weymouth Harbour.

From the Fort take one of a number of flights of steps down to the Nothe walk alongside the Harbour. One of these flights has an iron rail on each side. This was an inclined tramway for ammunition trucks serving the Fort in its early days. To the east is the stone pier protecting the harbour mouth.

Follow the tree-shaded promenade westwards past the yard and slipway of the Weymouth Sailing Club, then the Lifeboat Station and the delightfully varied terrace houses of Nothe Parade. No 2 dates from 1775; 3, 5 and 6 are of about 1810, and the others are Victorian.

A bridge crosses a slipway used for boat repairs. This is an old established yard, the slipmaster's house with its balustraded steps dating from about 1780. Nothe Parade runs into Hope Street. Despite its relatively modern appearance No 21 dates from the 16th century or earlier; no 22a, however, was built in 1977. Hope Street was once on the water's edge of the Ope, or cove, which ran back into what is now Hope Square and had houses on both sides, some right by the water.

The terraced cottages of Cove Row facing across the harbour date from about 1810 after the Ope was filled in about 1782. They were built to a design laid down by the local authority of the day - an early form of town planning.

Continue along the harbourside to the town pump, re-erected here and once an essential part of life in old Weymouth. Up Trinity Street is Trinity House, a fine Georgian brick building. Next to it is an Elizabethan town house which once backed onto the Ope. The sign over the door tells something of its history. Opposite is the classical Hope Chapel built in 1862.

And so to Trinity Road, immediately below Trinity Terrace and near the start of your walk. The elegant bow-fronted houses date from the late 18th and early 19th century. As the pavement beside the house nears the Town Bridge it ducks below road level and enters a tunnel under the steps of Holy Trinity Church. Here it is at the level of the old road before the bridge approaches were raised in 1824.

Holy Trinity Church when first built had its altar on the east wall and galleries set back on either side. When it was enlarged the altar was set on the south and two large transepts formed east and west. This unconventional solution has given us a fine interior. Just beyond the church are the steps which will take you up to Chapelhay and back to the starting point of your walk.

2. Harbourside and Old Melcombe Regis

We hope this walk will enable you to enjoy through its buildings a little of the history of this part of Weymouth which we shall be exploring within the grid pattern of streets of the medieval town.

Start at the Town Bridge and descend the steps to the quay below the Steam House Cafe. You are now standing on the old quay which met the water at the deep step above the present roadway and the railway line which was extended to the harbour in 1865. Until a few years ago flowers and vegetables imported from the Channel Islands were sent out along this line by goods train. Passenger trains continued to serve the Channel Island ferries until a few years ago and Weymouth was unique in having trains running on public roads.

Walk under the bridge and see two 18th century warehouses now converted to flats. Beyond them is the end of Nicholas Street and the site of the first bridge built in 1594 between Melcombe and Weymouth across the water. Before this, crossing was by rope-hauled ferry boat, when not disrupted by frequent feuding between the two communities. They had combined into a single borough in 1571. Imagine the harbour full of tall masted ships up to the old bridge. It was hereabouts that a trading vessel berthed in 1348 which is said to have brought the Black Death to England.

Return under the bridge which dates from 1930, being a rebuild of an earlier bridge of 1824. Cross to the harbourside walkway and proceed along Custom House Quay past the Royal Oak Inn (c 1840) and the Ship Inn on the corner of Maiden Street. Next see the Fish Market of 1855, built to enable local fishermen to market their catch more satisfactorily than on the quay side. In formal style with wide overhanging eaves, it is a building of distinction.

Go on to the corner of East Street where there is a fine red brick house with deep bow windows of 1800 or a little earlier. It was built by a merchant to enable him to oversee his shipping interests from his home; it is now the Coastguard HQ.

Opposite, the Diving Museum is in one of several warehouses, the present structures of which date from the early 19th century. They bear witness to the port's extensive trade with both Europe and America, especially in the 18th and 19th centuries. Despite some demolition most remain and have been converted to other uses. The chapel-like building housing the Royal Dorset Yacht Club (c 1866) was formerly a bath house for seamen, known as Sailors' Bethel.

At South Parade, No 14 Custom House Quay has bow windows on the corner. You will see during this walk how bow windows are a feature of the many late 18th century houses in the town. On the opposite corner, nos 15 and 16 are typical early Victorian cottages. Turn up South Parade looking into the narrow old street on your left on your way to the Esplanade.

Just ahead on the right the Alexandra Gardens are on the site of the medieval town midden or rubbish dump. In those days residents turned their backs on the sea but the late 18th century saw a recognition of its value and building began on this side with the terrace facing east across Alexandra Gardens. See some of the earliest sea front houses, nos 21 and 22 Esplanade, a little beyond your turning left into Belle Vue, a narrow old street with a selection of typical 18th and 19th century houses.

Before turning right up East Street, look left and you will see some fine Georgian houses (c 1780), notably nos 19-22 and 27. The Globe

Inn is a pleasant unspoiled Victorian pub. Beyond the car park and Market Street are nos 39-41 East Street, of about 1795; a most elegant group reminding us how much of the town looked before shopfronts were put in. Novelist and diarist Fanny Burney is reputed to have stayed here while covering the visits made by George III and his court to Weymouth.

Turn left and explore the delights of St Alban Street with its old fashioned bakery at the far corner. The oldest building here is the Milton Arms. Elizabethan in origin, it was a hostel for pilgrims passing through to Compostella in Spain. Here turn up New Street, "new" with its oldest cottages in the 16th century and having some interesting details at the southern end.

At the next junction is Upper Bond Street once a defensive ditch, the Cunigar, forming the northern boundary of medieval Melcombe between the sea and the inner harbour. At that time a sandy bar and rabbit warrens stretched north to Greenhill. Turning left we come to a wide junction with St Mary Street. Here the site of the old maypole is recorded in the pavement.

Turn left by Samuel's shop with its Victorian decorative ironwork and continue looking above the shopfronts at the varied architecture of former times. Can you spot the late Victorian Trocadero, one time restaurant serving cream teas and romantic music? Look into St Mary's church (James Hamilton 1817) with its reredos by Sir James Thornhill, a Dorset man, who painted the interior of the dome of St Paul's Cathedral.

Opposite is a brick arched entry into Rolls Court, once a group of cottages. To the left of St Mary's church once stood a covered market, and to the right on the corner of Church Passage stood a Tudor house. This was rebuilt in 1883 and some fragments of the old house were incorporated. The brackets in the gable once supported the bay windows of the old house. At the side entrance the 16th century canopy contains quaint supporting figures.

Continue and turn left into St Edmund Street. On the right is the collonaded classical Guildhall of 1837 containing the Council Chamber. The view is closed by the Methodist Church (Foster & Wood of Bath, 1867). To its left in Mitchell Street can be glimpsed the worthy Gothic Working Men's Club (G R Crickmay 1873). To the right the Duke of Cornwall is probably part of the early 17th century house which reached to the corner and is part of the range of buildings of that date which runs back to the quay and the Ship Inn. The Duke of Cornwall's elegant cast iron lantern was made in about 1845.

High in the gable opposite the church can be seen the point at which a cannon ball is said to have struck the building when fired from across the Harbour during the Civil War. This is probably true, as the stonework is damaged, but the ball apparently lodged there is a wooden replica.

You can now regain the quayside near the start of your walk.

Wimborne Minster

The market town of Wimborne Minster is almost encircled by the water-meadows of the Rivers Allen and Stour. In Saxon times, the town clustered closely round the Minster church, and even the medieval town was contained within its natural boundary, the River Allen. The shape of the present town was established by the 16th century. Considerable enlargement took place in the 18th century, when handsome Georgian buildings were constructed, mainly in East Borough and West Borough.

The Minster has always been the central point of the town and must be visited. The town trail starts from the north door: walk north-west into the Corn Market.

This enclosure of buildings was originally the central square of the town and the venue of the local market. Pigs were still being sold here in 1842.

On the north side is the Oddfellows Hall, erected in 1758 by the town's Friendly Society, and now a Heritage Centre. It has a Palladian window on the first floor and originally had open arcades on the ground floor. On the south side is the former George Inn, first recorded in 1524. The present building dates from the 18th century. Notice the signbracket above and the Venetian first floor window. The gates in the archway were erected by Wimborne Civic Society in 1982.

On the west is the White Hart, a 17th century timber-framed building — its low doorway showing how the street level has risen. The town's stocks, now in the Priest's House Museum, were situated outside here, and offenders were secured to a post inside the White Hart while they awaited punishment in the stocks. On the east side is

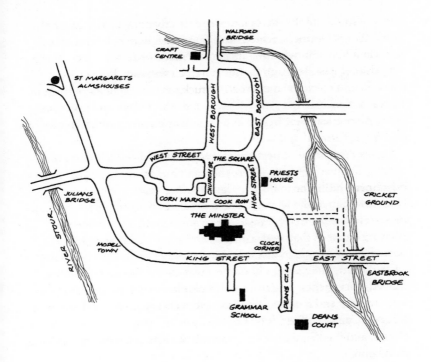

Tower House of three storeys, with an 18th century doorway with curved hood and an insurance plaque on the wall.

A lane from the north-west corner of the Corn Market leads to West Row, passing the Masonic Hall, converted from the town's first Methodist Chapel.

On reaching West Street, turn right towards the Square. On the left, No 30 has a Regency verandah, and No 31/32 a Georgian front of seven bays in traditional local red brick.

The Square was created in the early 19th century when the ruined medieval church of St Peter was finally demolished. On the west side is the King's Head Hotel, late 18th century, its facade reconstructed after a fire in the 1880s. On the north side, notice the 18th century windows on the first floor of the Portman Building Society, and the Lloyds bank building, 1870s Italianate. Next to it is a recent development which took the place of an old coaching inn.

Leave the Square via East Borough which leads from the north-east corner. On the right is Percy House with a five bay Georgian front. Next door is Dormers, which has a fine porch with columns, and at the rear a Venetian window. Its garden stretches to the River Allen. Opposite is East Borough Cottage, a small Regency house.

When you reach the main road, look across to Allendale, a substantial town house of 1823, now an antiques showroom and restaurant. The symmetrical west front has a large Doric porch fashionable at that time. Turn left and walk to West Borough.

This is Wimborne's finest street. Opposite you and a little to the right is Gulliver's House, where the infamous smuggler, Isaac Gulliver, made his home in his later law-abiding years. He became churchwarden of the Minster, and a tombstone bearing his name can be seen in the Baptistry. Walk southwards towards the Minster, noticing a pair of thatched cottages, and a fine building which was turned into a cinema in the 1930s and is only now being restored.

On the left, No 24 has a good door hood, and No 22 interesting rubbed-brick arches. The distinguished white building is now a Doctor's surgery and next to it is a late 18th century house of three storeys (Conservative Club). On the right are King's House, Dicken's House, and the Wimborne Club, early 19th century with an imposing stone porch.

The view to the south has been dominated by the tower of the Minster, drawing you back into the medieval town. Cross the Square and walk along Church Street. The partly pedestrianised area you have now entered is a maze of narrow medieval streets around the Minster. Church Street leads to the north door of the Minster church itself. Turn left at Cook Row, passing the Yew Tree Restaurant, a two-storeyed 17th century cottage.

On reaching the High Street walk a little way to the left to look at the Albion Hotel, with its coaching arch. It is the oldest surviving licensed house in the town. Next to it is the Priest's House Museum, a medieval building with early 17th and 18th century additions and originally one of four such houses for the priests at the Minster. It houses an important collection of local antiquities, both inside and in the attractive garden stretching down to the river.

Retrace your steps and follow the street as it bends left at Church House (1906). Ahead of you a footway passes Kings Court (1982) and leads into the Crown Mead shopping area. At the far end is a riverside walk by the Allen, with views over the cricket ground towards a stretch of dignified terraced houses and 'Lewens', one of Wimborne's most attractive 18th century houses. Follow the river southwards to reach Eastbrook Bridge, which was on the eastern boundary of the medieval town. The unusual handrail was retained when the bridge was widened. Turn right and walk along East Street. At the crossroads at Clock Corner the cottages on the north-east corner, now small shops, have curved brickwork and roof-lines.

Make a short detour down Deans Court Lane. Note the doorway on the right, the ornamental wyvern gateposts, and an interesting lodge at the end. This has a date of 1715 and a remarkable doorway and fanlight.

Deans Court is private: it is an early Georgian house on the site of the medieval deanery. The extensive grounds and gardens can be visited during the summer. In the walled garden is a vegetable sanctuary, the first in the country, where rare varieties are being saved from extinction.

Retrace your steps to Clock Corner and turn left into King Street.

On the left is the Methodist Church (1967), with a courtyard in front. Flanking the courtyard is one of the oldest domestic buildings in the town, a house of 16th century origin with half-timbered gable.

A few yards further west, Grammar School Lane leads to the former Queen Elizabeth's Grammar School, now converted to housing. The school originated in a chantry founded in Wimborne Minster in 1496 by Lady Margaret Beaufort, mother of Henry VII. (The Beauforts lived at Kingston Lacy and their splendid tomb is one of the finest monuments in the Minster.) The Chantry priest taught Latin and Greek, and after the Dissolution the teaching continued and the school was given a charter by Elizabeth I.

On returning to King Street, and crossing to the Minster to return to your starting point, there is a fine view of the south side of the church and the monumental freestanding sundial of 1676.

If you have time, go to the outskirts of the town to see Julians Bridge, which crosses the River Stour on the road to Dorchester. Built in 1636 and enlarged in 1844, it was originally a pack-horse bridge and has refuges for pedestrians corbelled into the parapets on both sides.

On the Blandford road are St Margaret's Almshouses, a group of

low thatched buildings which occupy the site of a medieval leper
hospital. The chapel which served the hospital now serves the
almshouses and parts of it date back to the 13th century.

Walford Bridge crosses the River Allen on the road to Cranborne.
The Craft Centre at Walford Mill offers a fine view of the seven
arches of this old packhorse bridge.

TRANSPORT

Bournemouth International Airport

North of Bournemouth, at Hurn. There is a viewing gallery situated on the terrace in front of the restaurant. It overlooks the apron area and provides an uninterrupted opportunity for photographs.

More than 100,000 aircraft a year, from Cessnas to Boeings, use the airport – almost one plane movement a minute during the 12 busy 'daylight' hours of summer.

Bovington Army Ranges – Tanks

Bovington Army Camp is the centre of tank activity, and some tank firings are open to public view. The programme is only produced two months in advance, and is frequently altered due to changes in the course training programmes. It therefore has to be a matter of 'pot luck'! If you are keen to see the tanks in action and take your chance (not during August), the public viewpoints are at: Bovington – Clouds Hill by Lawrence's Cottage and Gallows Hill on the Wool/Bere Regis Road; Lulworth – the Bindon viewing point, 1.5 miles west of East Lulworth village.

Lulworth Range firing information is published at short notice in the Bournemouth Evening Echo, the Western Gazette and Dorset Evening Echo.

Swanage Railway

Steam trains run on this private line between Swanage and Harman's Cross daily in the summer. Swanage Station is open to visitors, with a railway souvenir shop and a nearby picnic area for enthusiasts.

Keen train travellers may like to know that the Dorset Trust for Nature Conservation have joined with Network SouthEast to produce a free informative leaflet "Wildlife on the Line". This aims to draw your attention to habitats that can be seen in Dorset from your train, adding to the interest and enjoyment of your journey.

VILLAGES

Nearly every village in Dorset is picturesque, and most are best explored on foot. The following four are outstanding, and are worth a special trip to see. They are quite different in character.

Abbotsbury

The cottages are mostly of golden stone, and many are thatched. Abbotsbury used to be a fishing village, but is now very much a tourist attraction with the Swannery on The Fleet, and the nearby Sub-tropical Gardens.

Cottages of the 17th and 18th centuries line the main street, and there are some narrow corners for motorists. Visit the Church of St Nicholas, and climb the hill to St Catherine's Chapel for a beautiful view of the village and out to sea.

The Abbey Barn is still in use, and is one of the largest barns in England. Decorative stone from the ruined Abbey is evident in many of the walls throughout the village.

Cerne Abbas

This pretty village on the River Cerne is tucked in a cleft in the valley, overlooked on one side by the massive striding figure of the Cerne Giant.

The striking chalk carving is 180' tall and thought to be Romano-British in origin; possibly a representation of Hercules.

Long Street and Abbey Street contain examples of Tudor houses with their timbering and jettied upper storeys, 17th century cottages, and red brick Georgian houses. The Church of St Mary the Virgin is 15th century. The remains of the old Abbey can be seen, and a nearby spring is said to have been created by St Augustine.

Cerne Abbas used to boast a thriving leather industry, with Queen Victoria as a valued customer. When it was bypassed by the railway, however, the business slowly declined, and Cerne Abbas became the quiet Dorset village of today.

Abbey Street, Cerne Abbas.

Corfe Castle

An ancient stone village clustered at the foot of one of the most impressive ruins in the country. The castle guarded the only gap in the Purbeck Ridge, and has an unparalleled site. Corfe Castle was reduced to a ruin in 1646, finally falling to besieging Roundhead troops after being courageously defended by Lady Bankes during the Civil War.

The village prospered through working Purbeck Marble, which was used extensively for decorative internal features of buildings, particularly churches. It originated one of the oldest trade unions in the world – the Company of Marblers and Stone-Cutters of the Isle of Purbeck.

Note the Greyhound Hotel with its columned porch (1733) in the Square; see the Town Hall (1774), believed to be the smallest municipal building in the country; explore the narrow streets and the rows of 17th and 18th century cottages, roofed with Purbeck stone slabs.

Milton Abbas

The earliest mention of Milton Abbas, or Middleton as it used to known, is in the reign of King Athelstan who granted a market and fair to the town. In the Domesday Book the town belonged to the Abbey, and clustered close to it.

The present village, with its 'picture postcard' rows of thatched cottages lining the main street, was built in 1771-1786. The Earl of Dorchester, who was the landowner, ordered the old town surrounding the Abbey to be demolished and the site of the village moved further away. The lake at the bottom of the village was formed at this time; some householders who refused to sell their leases found their homes swamped when the Earl ordered the breaching of the dam that held the lake in front of the Abbey.

The Abbey Church is one of the finest in the county, and enjoys magnificent views over the surrounding Delcombe Valley.

Nearby St Catherine's Chapel, with its long approach of grass steps, is worth visiting. The steps are no longer in use, and the chapel must be approached from the Abbey/village road.